MANAGEMENT MAKEOVER

The Ultimate Guide
to MAXIMIZING Your
Property Management Income

Marie Hamling, CPM®
Property Rescuer℠

Copyright © 2017 by Marie Hamling. All rights reserved.

No part of this publication may be reproduced, stored in a retrieval system, or transmitted, in any form or in any means—by electronic, mechanical, photocopying, recording, scanning or otherwise—without the prior written permission of the author.

Limit of Liability/Disclaimer of Warranty: While the author has used her best effort in preparing this book, she makes no representations or warranties with respect to the accuracy or completeness of the contents of this book and specifically disclaims any implied warranties of merchantability or fitness for a particular purpose.

The methods described within this book are the author's personal thoughts. They are not intended to be a definitive set of instructions for any project. The advice and strategies contained herein may not be suitable for your situation. You may discover there are other methods and materials to accomplish the same end result. You should consult with another professional where appropriate.

The author has tried to recreate events, locales and conversations from her memories of them. In order to maintain their anonymity in some instances she may have changed the names of individuals and places. She may have changed some identifying characteristics and details such as physical properties, occupations and places of residence.

Published by White Door Publishing

Fort Myers, FL USA

800-345-4025

Cover design by Heather Perez and Jacob Hamling

Edited by Carol Cartaino

Images used under license from Shutterstock.com

Print ISBN: 978-1-48359-954-0

eBook ISBN: 978-1-48359-955-7

DEDICATION

*To my husband, Charlie.
This book was your idea and you lent encouragement
and hours reading and editing it.
Without you, I wouldn't have learned how
much fun it is to write and share.*

ACKNOWLEDGMENTS

Words cannot express my gratitude to Carol Cartaino, the best editor ever. Your enthusiasm, reassurance, and knowledgeable advice made this book happen. Your assistance was invaluable.

Thank you to Charlie, my husband, and all my friends and family for listening to me while I talked about writing this book, and for your constant encouragement and support while I was doing it.

I am grateful to Heather Perez and Jacob Hamling for the design of this book's cover.

A big thanks, too, to everyone across the country I have had the pleasure of working with. I have learned something from each and every one of you. I spent more time with some of you than I did with my family. I will never forget you.

TABLE OF CONTENTS

DEDICATION	V
ACKNOWLEDGMENTS	VII
INTRODUCTION	1
CHAPTER 1	7
ABOUT THIS BOOK	7
CHAPTER 2	12
I GET BY—OR DO I?	12
LET'S JUST USE A CAKE PAN—REALLY?	13
SLUMLORD	14
SPEAKING OF FINDING SOLUTIONS	17
PUT SOME PANTS ON AND DO YOUR JOB	18
DON'T TELL ME I CAN'T DO IT	19
IT'S WHAT YOU PUT INTO A NAME	24
PAY ATTENTION TO DETAIL	28
CHAPTER 3	31
PROPERTY MANAGEMENT VS. ASSET MANAGEMENT	31
CHAPTER 4	38
REAL ESTATE MANAGEMENT IS A SERVICE BUSINESS	38
SERVE YOUR CLIENTS	39
CUSTOMER SERVICE TO RESIDENTS, TENANTS, AND GUESTS	41
COMPASSION: THE CRUX	42
CHEERLEADERS: THE REINFORCEMENT	44
CUSTOMER SERVICE MADE SIMPLE	51
HIRE THE ATTITUDE	51
CHAPTER 5	54
STREAMLINING OPERATIONS TO MAXIMIZE RETURN	54

ARE THE RIGHT PEOPLE ON BOARD?	56
MAXIMIZE EFFICIENCY AND ELIMINATE UNNECESSARY COSTS	67
ANALYZE EXPENSES	70
ANALYZE REVENUE	75

CHAPTER 6 — 80
UNDERSTANDING YOUR NUMBERS — 80
IT'S ALL IN THE BUDGET	81
COMPARE APPLES TO APPLES—NOT APPLES TO ORANGES	87
DON'T JUST BE A CHECK SIGNER	91

CHAPTER 7 — 95
IMAGE IS EVERYTHING — 95
WHO DO YOU WANT TO BE?	96
WHAT'S IN A TITLE?	97
RESPECT YOURSELF!	100
DRESS TO IMPRESS	101
THE APPEARANCE OF PROMOTIONAL MATERIALS COUNTS, TOO	105
WHO DESIGNS THESE WEBSITES?	108
IT'S NOT THE RITZ—BUT IT CAN BE	110

CHAPTER 8 — 112
RISKY BUSINESS — 112
RISK MANAGEMENT AND INSURANCE COVERAGE	112
SURPRISE! HE'S YOUR STATUTORY EMPLOYEE.	117
WHAT WAS HE THINKING!	120
YOUR SOLUTION COULD BE A LAWSUIT IN WAITING	121
FIND A VERY GOOD INSURANCE AGENT	122

CHAPTER 9 — 125
HOW DO YOU MEASURE UP? — 125

ABOUT THE AUTHOR — 128
NOTE FROM THE AUTHOR — 130

INTRODUCTION

When I first thought of writing a book, I wanted to tell many of the stories I had from the years I've worked in real estate management, to help others become truly great managers or owners of their own business.

What happened is I began thinking about the relationships I've had that were created and molded over the years. I remembered little things people did or said that made a huge difference in my thinking. I recognized some things about myself I hadn't realized before. I became even more thankful for the sacrifices my family had made for me during my journey through the professional world. And I recognized that the love of my family and friends is what has sustained me.

I say all that because I can't write this book about improving your career without providing a glimpse of my personal side. It is who I am, how I work and play, how I form relationships, and how I teach others to improve. The chapters you will be reading contain many real-life stories, but from my perspective, of course. So it is all personal!

With me, what you see is what you get. I wear my emotions on my sleeve and say what I am thinking. What you get is a genuine person who cares about people, but will be firm when it comes to getting the job done.

My parents instilled the work ethic in me that has influenced my entire life. I grew up on a small farm in Colorado without modern conveniences and with very little money. Every member of the family was expected to contribute. There was housework to do, animals to feed, eggs to gather, fields to plow, and vegetables to pick from the garden.

If I didn't have something to do and my mom thought it was too early to play, I had to sweep the dirt yard with a broom. You see, we didn't have a lawn. We had the cleanest, least dusty dirt yard ever. Actually, I don't know that for sure, but none of my friends had to sweep dirt.

One day, a very successful friend and I were talking about how our humble upbringings formed us as adults. He told me he grew up in the ghettos of L.A. and all they had to play on was concrete. I answered back, "I grew up on a farm and we couldn't afford concrete." It makes me realize how different yet the same we all are. Doesn't matter whether you have to sweep dirt or concrete. Those who want to better themselves find a way.

Until the professional part of my life began, I thought everyone worked with the same fervor I did. I thought everyone put in a hard day's work and when it was all done, you went and played with your friends or spent time with family. I have learned that isn't exactly true.

I was talking with a real estate investor not long ago who told me what he thinks of property managers. He said you hire one, then you hire another and another until finally you settle for someone who seems to be the best of the worst. Why anyone would ever aspire to be only the best of the worst is beyond me. I was embarrassed to hear this.

What this book is about to unfold is how you can become one of the outstanding managers in your profession. Or if you are an employer, help members of your staff make you an exceptional property owner and make more money. I write about managing real estate because that is what I do. But I am talking to all managers and business owners who want to *stop* wasting their professional life and become more successful.

- ✓ **Do you or your employees do only enough work to get by?**

- ✓ **Are the financial results of your real estate assets mediocre and unexciting?**

- ✓ **Are you uncertain about the vision you should have for your real estate assets and how they should be performing?**

- ✓ **Are you or your staff indifferent to the needs of your customers and clients?**

- ✓ **Do you dive into a project without taking the time to thoroughly learn what it encompasses?**

- ✓ **Do you allow your staff to work blindly without knowing what you know, or at least have some idea?**

✓ **Do you stay in your safe, tidy little world without thinking outside the box?**

The good news is that making these mistakes *may* allow you to keep working in your present position for a long time. The bad news is that making these mistakes probably won't permit you to be a better manager or make more money, things that come to the elite in the business. You can do little, react to problems as they surface, and stagnate in your career or business; or you can chase your dream, enjoy more freedom, and make more money.

I don't care what anyone else says, we work to make money; whether working for someone else or for ourselves, whether living paycheck to paycheck or making millions every year. We all want to pay our bills and buy groceries. We like the simple comforts of electricity and running water; we need to be nourished; we want our vehicle to get from place to place, and we want to maintain the lifestyle of our preference.

If you are working for money, why be complacent when it comes to your professional life? If you think you aren't complacent, you should have answered "no" to every one of the above questions. Let's get to work to get smarter and better.

I have gained experience and wisdom from the people I've met and worked with. No one is too low or too high on the organizational chart to learn something from. I thank my lucky stars I've had the pleasure of spending time with all of these wonderful people. How much you listen to others is up to you. But if you think you can succeed all by yourself or that you know more than anyone else, particularly those who report to you, then you might as well stop reading now. I believe in the team concept and surrounding yourself with people who know more than you do, which this book promotes.

I assume you have completed at least some training and education in real estate management. Therefore, I am not going to fill this book with forms to use or directions on how to use them. I am not going to give you checklists to use to perform property inspections or obtain insurance coverage. I hope you have a clue as to what you are doing. I will tell you what you should be seeing and thinking while you are fulfilling your responsibilities. I want my journey through real estate management to help you grow and learn from real-life experiences. Don't settle for being the best of the worst. You can be the BEST of the BEST!

My husband is a retired truck driver who was on the road for many years. Truck drivers tell a joke that goes like this:

What is the difference between a fairy tale and a trucker's story? A fairy tale begins with "Once upon a time." A trucker's story begins with, "You ain't going to f#@#$*% believe this!"

So hang on to your hat and read on because this ain't no fairy tale!

CHAPTER 1
ABOUT THIS BOOK

Ask a child what he wants to be when he grows up and you will probably hear something like doctor, lawyer, firefighter, police officer, actor, pilot, teacher, astronaut, dancer, or musician. When was the last time you heard one say, "I want to be a property manager"?

Like many of those children, I went off to college to enter the medical field. Through happenstance, however, I ended up managing real estate and I've never looked back.

Many of us who manage real estate have fallen into it. I worked at a bank and met the gentleman who later hired me in his real estate management business. Some real estate investors start managing their own portfolio to make a little extra money. Some managers started in the business because they received a free apartment if they would maintain the property and collect rents.

When one falls into a job, what does one really know about it? From my experience, people who are starting in real estate management manage by winging it. Worse, there are even some who have been in the business for years plodding along, never learning any more than what they started with. This doesn't get them to the top of the pay scale though.

I have been managing real estate for many years and have hundreds of experiences to relate that will explain how to become one of the very best in real estate management. This book will take you through my journey with stories to teach you what I have learned. I will share personal relationships that have propelled me forward and the highs and lows of managing real estate worth millions of dollars.

Through the years, I have managed apartment homes, office buildings, single-family homes, manufactured home communities, hotel and executive suites, self-storage units, community associations, and RV parks. I have worked with Section 8 leases and other subsidized rent dwellings. In the hospitality sector, I managed a golf course, marina, and a general store. I have experience in home and lot sales. I have been a co-owner of a restaurant. Although this book focuses mainly on market rent multi-family and office building management, you will find other types of properties mixed in here and there. I believe if you love to learn, learn quickly, and are willing to keep updated on the latest information, you can manage whatever you put your mind to. You can when you seek and gain the knowledge to do so.

There are books on real estate management that cover the principles of management, along with forms and examples. Most are written for beginners in the business, landlords/investors, or classroom-type learning. There really isn't a book out there that takes a common-sense approach to specific situations real-estate managers face every single day, or that is entertaining and motivational as well as informative for those in the trenches working to become the best in the business.

This book is for those who are seriously interested in moving forward in what can be a very lucrative business. It takes a great attitude, initiative, hard work, a desire to help people and, above all, a willing heart—attributes this book will encourage.

I had been managing real estate in Colorado for almost twenty-five years when my husband and I decided to move to Florida. At that time in Colorado, a real estate license was required to manage any type of real estate: apartments, office buildings, condominium and homeowner associations (community associations), etc. I acquired a Florida real estate broker's license and thought I was set. Then I found out a separate license was needed for community association management (CAM). The prelude to applying and obtaining that license was taking an eighteen-hour class held over two days. I told my husband it only took eighteen hours, so he might as well attend with me and get his license. I hopped on the internet, found a company giving classes in our area, and signed us both up. We both passed the class, both passed the state test, and both obtained our CAM licenses. I was a bit jealous: I had twenty-five years of experience and he had a big fat zero years of experience. But after eighteen hours and a test, we both had a license to manage.

I have worked with some of the people, who like my husband, graduated from a two-day class and started managing. Oh, do they need help! That is where this book comes in. Classroom books, seminars, workshops, trade conferences, and all the rest tell students what their responsibilities will be and how to fill out forms, but so many don't tell them the rest of the all-important hows and even more important, the whys. What, How, and

Why make up the big picture of management. How does one manage millions of dollars' worth of assets if they can't see the whole picture?

The first owner I ever worked with told me I was a necessary inconvenience. He needed someone to manage his real estate assets, but he didn't want to have to pay them to do it. At least he was honest. Most owners of companies won't tell you that is how they feel—and many do feel that way! At the end of our working relationship, I had made him much more money than he ever paid me. I was only a necessary inconvenience for a brief time. That is what I want this book to impart to those serious about a real estate management career. Whether the owner is oneself or another, you have to work smart to create value for the owner. You must become an invaluable asset yourself.

The instructor for the CAM course I mentioned earlier had been managing real estate for almost twenty years for various management companies. While sitting in his class, I thought he must be an expert on how things were done in Florida. I asked several questions about Florida laws as related to specific areas of management, to which his response was, "I am not sure, but you don't need that for the test." They weren't difficult questions. After twenty years in Florida, the questions should have been easy to answer.

Over the past few years I've thought about this manager. I've wondered if he didn't want to learn more than what his company required or if it was the company's fault for not expecting more. One of the purposes of this book is to encourage managers to learn something new every day—to never stop learning and be resourceful in order to gain exceptional knowledge and skills.

If Only I Knew Now What I Knew When I Was a Teenager

I was behind a car at a stoplight many years ago and saw this on a sticker on its bumper. Think back to when you were a teenager. Ever wonder how adults in your world were able to function when they didn't know or understand as much as you? Funny how your parents became smarter as you got older. (It must have been your influence on them that helped them out!) My younger son started early. When he was ten he actually asked me how I ever graduated high school. I have to admit he is the most intelligent person I have ever met, but I am no slouch when it comes to intelligence.

I always wanted that teenage feeling again. To know everything. I study and research constantly. I act and make mistakes and learn from them. I've often said that when you make a hundred decisions a day they won't all be right. But make them and get on with your day; don't fall into the analysis paralysis trap. And when you've made a wrong decision, own up to it and learn from it so you won't make the same mistake again. A lesson learned helps you the rest of your life. Some of the best education comes from practical experience. I'll share mine, and I encourage readers to learn from the experiences of others. To be the best, surround yourself with the best—and learn from them.

CHAPTER 2
I GET BY—OR DO I?

It drives me crazy to work with someone who does just enough to get by, and never tries to do anything more. I was taught to strive to be the best at whatever I attempted.

The problem is, most managers don't even know they are working just enough to get by and some owners don't know they could have better. Then someone like me contacts the owner to let them know their asset could be managed at a higher level. And then the manager is gone, trying to convince another owner they can do the job and weren't fired because of their production.

If you are an owner of a company, pay attention to those who only get by. They are costing you money! And if you manage real estate for someone else, only getting by is *not* going to get you to the next level of compensation, particularly if it is based on the revenues of the owner's asset, which, by the way, you have probably been tasked with increasing.

When you aren't fulfilling your job to its greatest potential, you are actually increasing the probability of having problems that could have been avoided with capable oversight. When you do only enough to get by, you won't be ready for those problems when they do arise. Arm yourself with knowledge and do things right the first time so when there is an unavoidable problem, you can solve it quickly and correctly. There will be enough problems without you creating them by just getting by.

Many in real estate management believe that if something can go wrong, it probably will. Every day can bring a new horror story. Being prepared to handle whatever might go wrong is imperative.

LET'S JUST USE A CAKE PAN—REALLY?

A ceiling was leaking in an apartment of a large community that was a recently acquired management account. The maintenance crew cut the drywall in the ceiling, looking for a broken water line. What was found was a cake pan full of water sitting on the drywall under a pipe. Instead of repairing the leaking water line properly when it first leaked a couple of years earlier, the cake pan was placed under it to catch the water so it didn't leak through the ceiling. This worked for a while. Unfortunately, water finally filled the pan and it overflowed, causing the leak into the apartment. Know what my problem was? The maintenance person in charge who found the cake pan was the maintenance person who put it there in the first place.

This maintenance person had decided to do something easy to temporarily fix the problem. He was getting by and collecting his paycheck. This decision didn't serve him well in the end because he was now quickly terminated from his position. Unfortunately, the rest of the maintenance staff was subsequently terminated as well. They had also been taught to do a job to get by, and their attitude simply couldn't be changed.

The cause of this situation rested squarely on the shoulders of the community manager. She should have made sure her staff was properly trained. They should have been told what was expected of them. It sure wouldn't be to cut as many corners as possible so that things could be taken care of in the future. This was the time for Benjamin Franklin's "Don't put off until tomorrow what you can do today."

The manager should have been overseeing repairs and inspecting work done by the maintenance staff. Sure, you can't be everywhere all the time. But if your staff knows you will be inspecting repairs, they will be sure to complete them all properly. The manager is ultimately responsible. Leaving your staff without oversight doesn't even meet the "I'll get by" level of management.

I've heard other real estate investors and managers tell similar stories, so this is not a unique situation. Is it any wonder personnel issues pose one of the largest problems in running a business?

SLUMLORD

The owner of the real estate company I first worked with positioned his properties to be the best in the area in which they were located. I quickly embraced the concept and managed accordingly—best properties and highest rents.

So when we acquired an account from an investor who had recently purchased an apartment building I felt was a "slum," I was apprehensive. This was certainly an asset in distress where cash flow was nonexistent. It was one of the most difficult turnaround projects I had ever encountered.

During the initial inspection with the manager, we went into an apartment kitchen that had a space about two feet wide between the countertop and the range. I didn't understand this new design concept.

According to the manager, an electrical wiring repair had been made behind the wall, leaving a large hole in the drywall. The manager had been instructed by the investor to spend the minimal amount possible on repairs. To solve the problem of the hole, he simply moved the range over two feet to cover it.

The manager told me he showed the apartment, but no one wanted to rent it because there was no countertop next to the range. Well, excuse me, but isn't the purpose of a rental apartment to rent it? Who the heck doesn't complete a repair? This isn't just getting by; it is screwing the investor. This manager should have thought through the situation to find a reasonable solution. Instead, he approved the cost of the wiring repair because it had to be completed, but left another very minimal repair undone in order to save money. He took the direction to spend little too literally. He learned that not trying to find solutions might get you by, but it doesn't improve the condition or cash flow of an asset.

This is what we did to solve the problem. The hole in the wall was repaired at a very small cost, the range was moved back into its original space, the apartment was more thoroughly cleaned, and the apartment was rented. Simple. Since the condition of the apartment had been improved, we raised the rent twenty dollars per month. I shouldn't have to tell you nicer homes rent for more than those in poor condition, not to mention you acquire better residents.

A vacant home is generating no income. The longer it sits vacant, the less money there is to put back into the asset, the less money to pay the bills, and less money in the investor's pockets. This apartment rented quickly once proper repairs were done to make it market ready. Finally, it was generating income. And in two months, the increase alone paid for the repairs not previously completed. Yep, forty dollars was all it took.

The entire apartment building was cleaned, minor repairs made, and apartments were rented. Just getting by cost this investor big in the beginning. Doing the job right made him money in the end when the building was sold for significantly more than the purchase price.

Investors, if you aren't sure how to make this work for you, give me a call and we can talk about how I can help you streamline operations and make more money than you are making now. I am a turnaround specialist who has improved the bottom line for many assets.

Managers, it can be done! It's all in the effort you put into the task. Getting by won't get it done. Do some thinking, find solutions, and follow through with the appropriate solution.

SPEAKING OF FINDING SOLUTIONS

I feel compelled to share this story, although I am not particularly proud of it. An inspiring woman was promoted from a pool monitor position to the manager's assistant. She was then promoted to community manager. This in itself indicated that her job performance was impressive. Never having been a manager before, she needed training to learn all that was required. One very busy morning for me, she called to ask what I wanted her to do about a particular issue. After she told me the problem, our brief conversation went something like this:

> Manager: "What do you want me to do?"
>
> Me: "What should you have done instead of asking me that question?"
>
> Manager: "I shouldn't have called you."
>
> Me: "Not without recommending some solutions to the problem."
>
> Manager: "I'll call you back later."

That was absolutely not the right way for me to handle that phone call. Being busy is no excuse to be that abrupt with someone. I haven't forgotten it, because I made that manager feel badly. She didn't forget it either, because later she mentioned it numerous times. What it did, though, was teach her in about one minute that solutions should always accompany a problem.

True to her word, she called back later and I supported the solution she recommended. From then on, she always had solutions—good or bad ones—for the problems she encountered. There is always a solution. It may be to do something or it may be to do nothing, but there is one. Don't leave it up to someone else to figure out what needs to be done. That is only getting by.

PUT SOME PANTS ON AND DO YOUR JOB

The real estate management business requires oversight of contractors and various improvement projects. Be ready for this. Sometimes there will be an engineer or other professional who is responsible for inspecting and signing off on the completion of a project. However, there are times when you, the real estate manager, will be responsible.

A real estate manager in our company was overseeing the installation of a new shingle roof on a building in our management portfolio. This manager was an attractive woman who dressed for success on a daily basis. When the job was complete and the invoice received and approved by the manager, I asked her if she had inspected the roof prior to approving payment to the contractor. Imagine my surprise when she answered she had inspected it from the ground and it looked fine.

Go outside and look up at the roof of a two-story building and let me know what you see. I asked the manager why she didn't get on the roof, or at least on a ladder in order to see the roof. Her response was that she had on a skirt and heels so couldn't climb a ladder.

I started in this business when it was pretty much a man's world. I worked hard to prove myself and to gain respect for what I could accomplish. To be told she couldn't climb a ladder because she had a skirt on bugged the heck out of me. I too dress professionally for the office. But I am not going to get holes in the knees of my dress slacks or walk through the mud in my good shoes, so I carry a change of clothes in my car so I am ready to dig trenches or climb on roofs. And I am afraid of heights. When I climb a ladder to get on a roof, I have to have someone hold the ladder to keep it from falling over because I am shaking so badly. It doesn't stop me from doing my job, though.

When it is your job to inspect a contracted project, do it. Not having the proper clothing or the right kind of shoes doesn't give you the right to do the job halfway, or to do only what you have to in order to get by. There should be no excuses. You are a real estate manager! Put on a pair of pants, climb the ladder, and do your job! You owe it to the owners you represent. It is your duty to them.

DON'T TELL ME I CAN'T DO IT

My husband is a member of the Elks and we were very active in the local lodge for many years. Being a part of a fraternal, service organization has been one of the best experiences in our life. Brothers and sisters in arms, continually working for the benefit of others. The rewards to us from volunteering, giving and participating, were tremendous; the love and the friendship from the people around us the most incredible of all. I believe everyone should do what they can to give back, however, that is a topic for another time.

Every year a group of us built a float for the County Fair Parade to raise awareness of the Elks and its assistance to the communities it serves. It was long, hard work but a lot of fun as well. Almost every year, the Elks' float brought home a trophy. That's how much thought and work went into each one. One year, the theme of the fair was "*It's a Family Affair.*" A Fair—get it? And what is one of the biggest thrills at a fair but rides!

At our first meeting to discuss the float, one of the popular ideas was to build a float with a Ferris wheel as the focal point; a working Ferris wheel that went round and round every minute of the parade. We were getting very excited about this when one woman chimed in with, "You can't do it. The mechanics won't work." A few thoughts went through my mind. I am not going to put them in writing, but the one shouting at me was, "Don't tell me I can't do it!" I will do whatever possible to prove someone wrong when they tell me I can't do something. It is a dare I have answered more than a few times in my life.

My friend and I looked at each other knowingly and we told the group that not only could we do it, we would do it. And that was that. No one even called for a vote. The float was going to have a working Ferris wheel. We started planning at that very moment.

We got up, went into another room with another group of members, and walked up to Jim and Jerry, who worked at IBM and Ball Aerospace respectively. We knew that with their engineering minds, these two could build anything and make it work. We told them what we wanted and they looked at us like we were crazy, but told us they would work on it. I don't think these poor guys knew what they were getting into when we happily skipped away and left the Ferris wheel in their hands. The rest of us planned and designed the rest of the float.

Jim and Jerry spent hours and days coming up with a way to make the Ferris wheel go round and round. They had to build the wheel in such a way that all the moving parts worked together. They brought the wheel, which was approximately ten feet high, to us so we could put the finishing touches on it and make it pretty. Then we all got together for the first test. The motorized mechanisms were plugged in and attached to the wheel. We decided someone had to ride the ride, so we put stuffed animals and dolls in the seats of the wheel. The motor was turned on and the wheel started turning. We started cheering and jumping up and down. But the wheel started going faster and faster and faster. The next thing we knew it was chaos! The stuffed animals and dolls were thrown from the wheel and scattered all over the yard. Whoops! Back to the drawing board.

The guys did it, though. Jim had built the drive with a lawn mower transmission and had to rearrange the pulleys to slow it down. (Maybe those cartoons with a lawn mower running away from the user were based on true stories?) A few days later, a second test was done and the final product worked perfectly. That

Ferris wheel never stopped turning at just the right speed during the parade. With our people in fair attire, clowns entertaining the spectators, the music, and the accompanying decorations, that float was flawless in our eyes. Perhaps in the eyes of others as well, because we took home the Grand Prize trophy.

Are you thinking, "What does this have to do with improving and making more money in my career?"

All of those involved in this project were people who worked in a broad scope of professions, including accounting, design, engineering, management, secretarial work, carpentry, teaching, metalworking, and logistics, to name a few. Yes, we brought our work experience to what we did in our leisure time, but it was still work. Each and every one had a "can do" attitude. We were all surrounded by others who had strengths to overcome the weaknesses of others. When asked for help, each and every one provided the help. We worked together and made great things happen. Isn't this what we are supposed to try to do every day at work?

Your team shouldn't consist of only people who are employed by your company, but the contractors and professional services who work with you. You should be surrounding yourself with landscapers, general contractors, electricians, plumbers, engineers, attorneys, IT and marketing teams, etc., who want to work with you to meet the goals of the property.

It doesn't matter if you are working on a float for fun or working to put some money in your pocket, it takes good people working together to be successful. Think of what can happen if you surround yourself with knowledgeable, goal-oriented people and the entire team believes there are no bounds to the possibilities of what it can accomplish!

Are you one who thinks the glass is half full, or more likely to think of it as half empty? The woman at the meeting who said we couldn't build a working Ferris wheel must have been the latter. I don't know if she was embarrassed or angry or what, but she never came back to help with the float. She removed herself as the weak link in an optimistic team. If we had believed her, though, we could have gotten by and still had a good float. We would have had a Ferris wheel that didn't go round and round, but it would have still looked nice. Yes, we would have gotten by. That isn't good enough for me, it wasn't good enough for our float team, and it shouldn't be good enough for you. There is always a next level that you should try to attain. Look at the glass as half full and you are on your way to achieving the next level.

Optimism, confidence, perseverance, caring, and passion make anything possible. Live life with the attitude that you will succeed and not just get by. It will come naturally when you go to work.

Don't tell me I can't do something. I guarantee I will do what it takes to show you I can. Getting by isn't in my vocabulary and it shouldn't be in yours.

IT'S WHAT YOU PUT INTO A NAME

Real estate management is a sales business. Every time someone requests information about a home, room, unit, or space to rent, the sales process begins. The goal is to get them to sign a lease and you have to sell the idea to them. The monetary commitment made by someone signing a lease can be as large as purchasing a car or a home. An annual lease for an apartment at $1,500 per month is $18,000 per year. The annual commitment for office space at $5,000 per month is $60,000 per year. If they sign a five- or ten-year lease, that equates to $300,000 to $600,000 over the life of the lease. Yes, you are selling something valuable.

And then there are some in the business who actually sell the product; homes and home sites. I've never understood why the people in this type of sales receive more sales training than those selling leases.

I have created and implemented training programs for companies for years and most of those programs include sales. When I train managers and leasing consultants in sales, more apartments are rented and more leases are renewed. The change in attitude towards selling something creates excitement and produces positive results. The only time I can think of that a manager does not have to think about selling to a renter is when the rental market is so robust all they have to do is answer the phone and the space or home is rented. That market isn't going to last forever and you should know how to sell when it isn't so good and you have to work to get a lease signed. When the phone rings in a bad market, you had better make sure the person who answers is selling the property and gets an appointment to tour the property, or you have lost the prospect to someone else.

A few years ago I was leading one home sales team out of four in the company. For the most part, members of each team were spread out over several states. I had ten sales managers in seven cities in four states.

The head of the entire sales division decided each team needed a name to increase competition and, thus, increase sales. It was my job to come up with a name for the team I directed. We were having a contest!

A couple of hours after I received the initial notice to name the team, I received a communication asking if I had a name yet because the other teams had already submitted theirs. Heck, I was still deliberating, trying to find the name that would instill some excitement in my team. Why could everyone else come up with a name quickly when it was taking me so long? I was second-guessing myself. Don't do this to yourself! You'll understand why in a few paragraphs.

Even though it took me a day longer than anyone else to submit a name, I took my time, putting great thought into it. I sent the name I chose to each of the ten sales managers and asked for their opinion and comments. I won't go into all the detail because there was a lot of it. Suffice it to say the name was well liked and all approved. We adopted it. It was:

The F.O.R.C.E
(Focused on Retailing and Competitive Excellence)

Come on, I had to come up with something to go with the abbreviation.

I eventually found out why it took me so much longer to come up with a name. The other names were things like Rhoda's Gang, Mike's Group, and The R&Rs. Unbelievable. It would have also taken me only about thirty seconds to come up with Marie's Troop. But no, I wanted something the sales team could grab on to and relate to. Something that got the competitive juices flowing. Something that made them go out and sell more. The team became the F.O.R.C.E. Wouldn't you rather be part of a FORCE than part of someone's group or gang?

One of the sales managers on our team was at a store in Orlando and saw a miniature Darth Vader figure. She bought enough for the whole team and mailed them off to everyone. Remember, these people weren't all in the same state and didn't see each other often. She didn't care. They were part of her team and she thought of a way to bring them all together by giving them a tiny Darth Vader.

Now everyone had something to look at to remind them what the job was and we had an internal logo too. Every piece of correspondence between us had the logo and name at the top. Each manager always had their F.O.R.C.E. Darth Vader on their desk by the phone. We had a sales meeting and every manager brought their Darth Vader and put it on the table in front of them. They were absolutely into being the FORCE in sales.

The F.O.R.C.E
LeventKonuk/shutterstockinc.

I was so proud of the sales team I worked with. They embraced the challenge with enthusiasm and confidence. They were part of the decision to name themselves, they wore the name with pride and they never looked back. They became a FORCE to be reckoned with.

Guess which team won the contest? Yep, the F.O.R.C.E.

You see, I believe a thirty-second name is only getting by. It takes no thought, no planning, and no creativity. The reason for the name was to drive the team. Our name even had a meaning; it stated what our focus was. Our team wasn't Marie's team. It was the team for all; it was a F.O.R.C.E. The members all wanted to do better for themselves, not for me.

Getting by with one of those thirty-second names might have made the contest more fun, but it didn't necessarily achieve the goal—*Sell More*! Getting by doesn't sell more product, get to the next level, or put more money in your pocket. Achieving the next level is a lot more fun than getting by, believe me.

PAY ATTENTION TO DETAIL

My husband tells me continually that he is amazed at what I see when I walk into a room. I see the smudge on the wall, the stain on the carpet, the tiny nail hole, a spot on the tablecloth, or the dirty window that no one else notices. When I inspect a property, I find issues that are glaring to me that have been overlooked or ignored by those working on the property. This comes naturally to me. If it doesn't come naturally to you, I believe you can train yourself to do the same.

Our company was hiring a property manager and I was interviewing a woman who managed a nice hotel. I met her at the hotel she managed. After the introductions, she wanted to show me the pool area so we walked from the front office, around a few buildings, to the pool. Along the way, I picked up several pieces of paper, three or four cigarette butts, a juice box, and a soda can. By the time we got to the waste can outside the pool gate, I had two handfuls of trash to throw away. The manager never looked down and not once stooped down to pick up debris that didn't belong on or along the sidewalk because she didn't see it. I looked at the pool area, said my goodbyes and left. The interview, along with my interest in the manager, was over.

Another time, I walked into an office with a false ceiling made of fiber tiles. There was a water spot on two of them, so I asked the manager about the problem. His answer was, "I hadn't noticed the spots." The spots were dry so this didn't just happen the day I got there. It turned out that a small leak in the roof had made its way to the ceiling during a rain a few days earlier. No one looked up to see the water spots, though.

On another occasion, I was driving through a property with the facilities manager to inspect the maintenance area when I noticed two reflectors on crooked metal posts stuck in the ground in a common area. When he stopped the cart as requested and I looked at the spot where the reflectors were, there was a hole in the ground about six inches wide and ten inches deep. I assumed that whomever had found the hole marked it with the reflectors, but didn't report it to the management office. I asked the facilities manager about it and he told me he hadn't noticed the reflectors. They were an eyesore, so I didn't understand how they could be missed. If he had looked around while walking and driving through the property, he would have seen them and then would have made the necessary repairs to eliminate the safety risk the hole presented.

You have to look down, you have to look up, and you have to look around to notice what is happening. Up, down, and around. Look everywhere.

There are great managers out there who see everything and respond. One day I performed an inspection at a community with almost seven hundred homes. In the community's common areas, clubhouse, recreational areas and all those homes, I did not find one single issue to point out or write down. Not one. What a day!

Don't only focus on the immediate job you have to do. There is a bigger world (or property issue) than the light bulb that needs to be changed, the room that needs to be painted, the faucet in the restroom that needs to be repaired, or the space that needs to be rented. While you are on your way to do what is needed, pay attention to everything else along the way. When you don't pay attention to all the details, you are getting by, but you won't achieve the level of success you are seeking.

To do more than get by, you need to do things right the first time, put some thought into what you are doing, be prepared, work with the awareness that there is a solution to every problem, and pay attention to every detail. When you pay attention to detail, the maintenance tech is not going to be using a cake pan to catch drips, or moving a range to cover a hole in the wall. When you pay attention to detail, you are going to be ready to oversee and inspect any project there is. When you pay attention to detail, you are going to find a solution to any problem and you are going to make sure your promotional ideas are going to attract business. When you pay attention to detail, getting by is no longer in your vocabulary. Hello, bigger paydays!

CHAPTER 3
PROPERTY MANAGEMENT VS. ASSET MANAGEMENT

Before we go any further, we need to discuss real estate **property** management and real estate **asset** management. There is a difference you should understand.

Property management and asset management are two different professions.

Property management can be a career path to asset management, but rarely is one able and/or willing to make the transition. It could, however, be a twenty percent to forty percent differential in compensation according to information gathered by the

Institute of Real Estate Management. What could you do with an extra twenty percent to forty percent in income?

Property management concentrates on the day-to-day operations of a property. People who work at specific properties are typically fulfilling property management responsibilities. Property management includes, but is not limited to:

- Maintenance of the property and facilities

- Renting dwellings, sites, rooms, etc.

- Collecting rent and other charges

- Working with staff and contractors

- Dealing with resident, tenant, and guest issues

- Enforcing rules, regulations, covenants, and guidelines

- Risk management

Over the last decade or so, property management began to change and it continues to evolve. While there are still some "old school" property managers who think their only responsibilities are to maintain the property and collect the rent, the evolving property managers are acquiring the responsibility for financial analysis and making recommendations based on the financial impact to the property. They prepare annual budgets and work toward improving the net operating income of a property. But this does not make them asset managers.

Asset managers understand real estate as an investment. Asset management is centered on financial matters: maximizing the return on investment and the value of property. They are adept at streamlining operations and repositioning a property to reduce costs and increase income. Quite simply, they find ways to increase revenue, decrease expenses, and increase the value of a property.

Asset management includes tasks such as:

- Preparing long-term financial forecasts and cash flow analysis, and computing internal rate of return in order to determine a property's financial performance

- Performing due diligence (detailed investigation) for acquisition or disposition of property and providing recommendations

- Determining the highest and best use of the property

- Determining the value of a property and what can be done to increase the value

- Finding and working with lenders

- Negotiating on behalf of the owner

- Marketing an asset to increase revenue

Asset managers can oversee ten to thirty properties. They typically manage at the portfolio level, making sure operations at the individual property level are running smoothly and correctly.

There are asset managers who are very involved at the property level, but there are also some who are not. Much depends on the environment of the company in which they work.

Most real estate managers are either a property manager or an asset manager. In my opinion, the best real estate managers know how to perform both jobs, or at least a little bit about the other's job. Remember when I said *What*, *How* and *Why* make up the big picture of management? Helping investors meet their goals is *Why* you are managing their assets, knowing *How* to reach those goals and *What* to do to get there makes you successful.

As an asset manager, how do you maximize return and value if you don't understand what it takes to enforce rules, collect rents, deal with contractors, or handle issues with residents, tenants, or guests? My suggestion is to spend a week on-site and find out what property managers put up with on a daily basis. You might actually find new ways to create efficiencies to maximize return.

How does a property manager understand how to maximize return and value for an investor if the only thing he or she knows is how to manage day-to-day operations? One can manage a property without understanding its financial condition, but this isn't ideal for the investor who wants to make as much money as possible.

Our corporate office needed someone to answer the phones and perform administrative work for a few days while the person who normally did this took a few days off. It was arranged for a property manager at a community to fill the need. Later, she told me this was one of the best experiences she'd ever had because she was able to see a little bit of what went on in our office as opposed at the property level. "I wondered what you did all day," she said. "Now I have a much better idea." It also made her want to learn more and improve as a property manager.

If you are a property manager and don't understand what an asset manager does, or if you are an asset manager and don't know what a property manager does on a daily basis, then find out. It makes the person in either position better. This is my personal belief based on interactions with both over the years. Feel free to agree or not, but in my mind, this is a fact.

There are more and more educational opportunities for property managers to move to the next step on their career path—asset management. However, as noted earlier, there are very few property managers who make this transition. If you don't choose to be an asset manager, you can still be an excellent property manager with more skills than most if you continue to educate yourself. Align yourself with a mentor who is willing to teach you how to improve your skill set. Make yourself needed and wanted.

Managers, it takes more education, perseverance, and a lot of hard work to move to the next level in your career. Today's real estate manager is evolving. Don't be left behind!

Real estate investors, ask yourself the following before hiring a manager or a management company:

1. Am I only concerned with the day-to-day operations of my property? (Property Management)

2. Am I only concerned with increasing income and/or eventually selling my property for more than I paid for it? (Asset Management), or

3. Do I want my property managed *and* to realize a maximum return on my investment and the value of the property? (Property Management and Asset Management)

When you know the result you want, you will be better able to ask the right questions and hire the right type of management for your assets. The following table shows what I believe to be the responsibilities and skills through the evolution of property managers and how they compare.

Real Estate Asset Management
Lists of Responsibilities/Knowledge

PROPERTY MANAGER	EVOLVING PROPERTY MANAGER	PROPERTY/ASSET MANAGER
Leasing/Sales	Leasing/Sales	Leasing/Sales
Maintenance	Maintenance	Maintenance
Administration	Administration	Administration
Computer Skills	Computer Skills	Computer Skills
	Management Skills	Management Skills
	Financial Budgeting	Financial Budgeting
	Income & Expense Statements	Income & Expense Statements
	Procurement Purchasing, bids, suppliers	Procurement Purchasing, bids, suppliers
	Risk Management	Risk Management
	Capital Improvements	Capital Improvements
	Market Surveys	Market Surveys
	Knowledge	Knowledge
	Recreation Facilities and Programs	Recreation Facilities and Programs
		Insurance
		Due Diligence
		Contract Negotiation
		Personnel – Human Resources
		Advertising & Marketing
		Feasibility Studies
		Accounting
		Construction & Design
		Policy & Procedures Creation & Implementation

CHAPTER 4
REAL ESTATE MANAGEMENT IS A SERVICE BUSINESS

We have an obligation to make sure the service we provide satisfies our clients and customers and meets their needs. Our **clients**, those who hire us to manage their real estate assets, expect us to maintain high-quality assets and produce the highest possible return on their investment.

Residents, tenants, and guests are our **customers** (which, for simplicity, is what I will call them in this chapter). Without them, there would be no business. And without a business, there is no investor to hire you. Thus, we must create customer loyalty through exceptional customer service in order to meet the needs of our clients.

This all begins with a basic operating **attitude**. Treat clients and customers honestly and professionally. Show respect and empathy. Be responsive and positive. And always smile!

So how do we put this altogether?

SERVE YOUR CLIENTS

When I became a member of The Institute of Real Estate Management, I agreed to abide by its Code of Professional Ethics. The Member Pledge includes the following:

I pledge myself to place honesty, integrity, and industriousness above all else and to pursue my gainful efforts with diligent study and ongoing education so that my services shall be beneficial to the general public and my obligations to my clients shall always be maintained at the highest possible level.

I believe if you are serving clients, you are obligated to follow the same code regardless of whether you are a member of an association or other group or not. In Real Estate Management 101 you learn one of your basic responsibilities is to meet the goals and objectives of the owner. Your services to your clients should *always* be maintained at the highest possible level.

You have a fiduciary responsibility—a special relationship of trust, confidence, and responsibility—to your clients. You must always remain loyal to your client and act in his or her best interests.

An associate of mine, Gary, had a small apartment community in his management portfolio that was owned by an older woman. She was one of the neediest clients I have run across and she required a lot of handholding. Because it was her only real estate investment and it was the income supplement for her retirement, she was very attentive to the investment and wanted frequent updates on it.

Gary is a very compassionate man who cares deeply for people. For many years, he spent an inordinate amount of time helping the owner and managing her asset at a high level because he cared about her. This small asset took as much or more time to manage as much larger ones. But because the management fee was based on revenue, the fee would always be lower than a larger property of the same type.

Gary's oversight of this asset went above and beyond normal expectations. The asset generated good cash flow for the owner and, after her death, for her children. Gary served his client with loyalty and care and at the highest possible level for many years. She trusted him implicitly. He didn't base his service on the amount of fees he was paid and he didn't reduce his service because he didn't have time for it. If you are going to agree to serve a client, give them the best service possible to maintain the asset in exceptional condition and generate the most income for them, as Gary did.

I am not implying you should seek out accounts like this one that could lose you money. But if you do accept them, serve your clients well regardless. This attitude may lose you money on an individual case, but it can make you money in the long run by producing sincerely positive testimonials from an owner, and then you can use your confidence and enthusiasm on larger projects that make more money. What goes around, comes around.

CUSTOMER SERVICE TO RESIDENTS, TENANTS, AND GUESTS

Let's repeat this—if there are no customers, there is no business to provide a return on your client's investment. You can care about your client all day long, but if you don't care about the customer, it's not worth a hill of beans. To rise to the top in your chosen field, it is going to take unsurpassed customer service; service that exceeds expectations. Customer service isn't only about making a good first impression. We want to attract and then retain customers for the real estate assets we manage.

Customer service is always having a pleasant attitude to all alike. It is always providing timely responses. It is always having a caring, helpful attitude. It is always being fair and uniform. This one is very important. Be uniform in all your actions and interactions. You should uniformly enforce rules, uniformly maintain policy, and uniformly treat everyone the same. When your actions are uniform, you reduce the risks of playing favorites and unfair treatment that can lead to Fair Housing issues.

I am going to call a person who provides unsurpassed customer service a "Compassionate Cheerleader." (I told someone the other day I could only be their cheerleader, so I like that word today.) Quite frankly, I believe if you can't be a Compassionate Cheerleader, you probably shouldn't be a real estate manager, especially if you want to be one of the best.

COMPASSION: THE CRUX

A compassionate person cares sincerely and is kind, considerate, and generous. A compassionate person truly wants to help others. Your customers can sense whether you want to help them or not.

"Sincerely" is the optimum word here. A naturally sincere person treats everyone the same. Consider the manager who was smiling and making a good impression on her customers in the front office and the next minute charged out the door to yell and scream at a coworker that he wasn't doing his job correctly. All in front of other customers and noticed by the customers in the office. What are these customers going to remember? A nice welcome or the manager who yells at a team member? Based on subsequent comments and remarks, it was *not* the nice welcome. This was not the kind of unsurpassed customer service the manager intended to give.

When a person is sincerely compassionate, it shows in everything he or she does, including the day-to-day operations of a property. I was tasked with cleaning up a large community of manufactured homes. The place was a scary mess. Most of the residents didn't have a lot of money to put back into their homes. But that really wasn't the problem. There was trash, debris, and non-working vehicles everywhere on the sites. And the common areas were dismal.

The first thing I did was replace the Community Manager with a man who was previously a Regional Director for an apartment management company. As the new Community Manager, he subsequently hired new staff. Now everyone was on the same page—cleanup of the community. To entice residents to clean their sites and comply with community guidelines, we began by drawing up plans to install new landscaping and fencing at the front entrance, along with a few other minor improvements. The new manager was given a budget and the go-ahead to proceed with the improvements.

During each of my visits I noticed improvements, not only in the common areas of the community but in the condition of the residents' sites. The visit at the end of the project, though, was the best. The new manager used money realized from cost-saving measures on the landscape budget to plant new landscaping in other areas as well. He gave plants to residents for their yards and greatly improved the exterior appearance of the community center. In addition, he helped the residents to remove the debris around their homes. All this within his original budget.

When I expressed my appreciation and excitement to the manager, his reply was, "Everyone deserves to live in a quality community. I did all the extra work for them." And when he provided a higher quality community to his residents, they in turn took more pride in their residences. His belief that everyone deserves quality generated resident pride and loyalty.

His compassion for his residents completely turned the community around. He is one of the best!

And in the end, the turnaround of this community met the needs of the client. Existing residents were happier and stayed in the community because their needs were considered. The more attractive, better-managed community attracted new residents, which increased revenue. The community was maintained on a leaner budget while still eliminating deferred maintenance items. The value of the community increased and it was sold at a substantially higher price than would have been realized prior to the turnaround.

CHEERLEADERS: THE REINFORCEMENT

Cheerleaders are generally enthusiastic and outgoing, they have fun, they smile, they hardly ever stop moving, and they support their team. They cheer when things go right and they cheer with encouragement when things need to get better. And they are almost always optimistic. Cheerleaders don't leave the game when the score is 60-0. They keep on cheering, knowing their team can surely score more than 0. This is how we need to be with our customers.

I was a cheerleader in high school. Our team let us down on occasion by losing, but we never let our team down. You may occasionally feel a customer has let you down when they don't pay their rent or follow the guidelines of a property. You can't let them down, though. As a Compassionate Cheerleader, you still have to be kind and caring and you have to enthusiastically cheer them on to make things right. When they can't, you can still show empathy although you may have to take legal steps to remove them from a property.

As a cheerleader, you cheer them on when they do everything right and show you are pleased they are your customer. Show appreciation and say thank-you for being a good resident or tenant. Say "Have a great day" when you pass them, put a nice thank-you note on their door once in a while, or stop in and ask if everything is okay.

There was a branch office of a national corporation in a Class A office building in my portfolio. The manager of that office was one of the most demanding tenants I ever experienced. Overall, however, the company was a great tenant. When the manager made a request, I always responded quickly and with a good attitude. I thanked him for taking good care of their office space as often as he thanked me for fixing one of his problems. We had an enjoyable, successful, long-term relationship. That is what a happy customer gives you.

There you have it—a Compassionate Cheerleader. Someone who has a great positive attitude and sincerely cares about his or her customers.

While you and your team are being Compassionate Cheerleaders, remember the following. You can attract and retain more customers. It's all about customer service.

Stay Positive. Have fun, smile at everyone, and show enthusiasm. It's harder to complain or be negative or rude when you are enjoying yourself.

A positive person is more tolerant of others. If you have a customer who is angry or misbehaving in some way, ask yourself if there may be something unpleasant going on in their life to make them unhappy. You may never know how much your tolerance and understanding may help them at that moment and it will often keep a situation from going from bad to worse. A positive person finds something good in others. When you are positive, your customers will respond to *you* more positively.

My cousin, Carla, was more like a sister to me than a cousin. I was living with her when she was diagnosed with Lupus. I saw her suffer with this disease for many years. She spent the last six months of her life in the hospital, away from her husband and young daughter. Most of her days were agonizing for her. Every few days, the doctors would "wash" her blood. In layman's terms, this meant moving a portion of her blood through a machine where it was treated and then put back into her body. My understanding was that this wasn't a very fun thing to go through.

I was visiting her once right after one of these procedures. When I asked how she was doing, she told me she was having a great day. I was happy to hear this, and being the optimist I am, I was already asking if she would be able to go home soon. She looked at me then and with a smile said, *"You need to understand—my best day is like the worst day you have ever had."* That was a sucker punch I feel to this day. Still, she was smiling and happy to be alive.

When I am having a bad day or not feeling well, I think about Carla and know my day could be far worse. So if whatever is going on is the worst thing for me today, there are others who are having an even worse day. And this too shall pass.

Life's too short—**be happy**.

Be Respectful. Respect and show consideration to your customers. Use the other person's name, look them in the eye, and nod to show you understand what they are saying. Give your customers your undivided attention when on the phone. Don't work on something else even if you think the person on the other end of the line doesn't know that you are. Don't just treat customers the way you wish to be treated, treat them the way they want to be treated.

Show Empathy. Customers want to know you care. They want you to understand what they want and why they want it. They want you to respond to them. Service them with caring concern. Ask yourself how you would feel if you were in their position.

A customer is going to trust you much more if they believe you care about them.

Treat customers with courtesy and kindness. It is difficult to build a positive relationship with someone when you don't really care about them. You must still hold firm when following procedures and the law, but this doesn't mean you can't care about a customer and try to help them.

Know Your Job. It is much easier to provide unsurpassed customer service when you know what you are talking about; when you are confident in yourself and your decisions. Learn everything you can about the real estate management business or whatever business you have chosen. Learn something new every day.

- Keep up to date on the laws and regulations in your area.

- Participate in continuing education and training seminars.

- Read books and other publications that are specific to your business.

- Learn from everyone you work with.

- Join an industry association and benefit from its learning resources.

When you know your job, you can make decisions and respond more quickly to a customer. Your customers will respect you when they believe you are a professional who knows the business.

Communicate Effectively. Good communication skills are very important in helping us satisfy customers and prevent misunderstandings. To be an effective communicator, you need to **listen** first. A customer won't "hear" you listening, but you may actually hear what your customer is trying to say to you. Don't think about what you are going to say until you have listened to what the customer is saying to you. Stay focused on the customer's problem, perceived or actual, not on how loud the customer is yelling. When you understand the problem, it is much easier to find a solution.

It is possible your customer's view of a problem is different than the one you have. Ask them for their ideas or solutions to the problem. Sometimes they simply want to get the problem off their chest and all is well again.

I worked with a general manager who gave something away every time there was a complaint so there wouldn't be an argument. He gave free rent or utilities, gift certificates, show tickets, etc. He didn't know how to have a positive discussion and listen to a customer in order to come up with solutions to problems. I was in a meeting with him and an unhappy customer one day. Once the customer had angrily described his problem and before the general manager could offer something of value, I asked the customer what he would like us to do for him. I understood his dissatisfaction was due to a utility problem, but it had already been repaired. He said, "I just want an apology." He received one. He was satisfied because we listened to him and cared enough to ask what he needed. The only thing the customer was interested in was the apology—and that was free.

You need to be clear and concise when you communicate with customers. They have to understand what you are telling them. Make sure you know what you are saying—another reason to know your job. If you are not certain what you are saying, your customer isn't going to understand it and they will most likely stop listening to you.

There was a time I received numerous phone calls from residents of a multi-family property complaining about the on-site manager. He was trying to enforce the covenants of the community and making almost everyone angry when he spoke with them or sent them a notice. They didn't understand his directives so they stopped listening to him and called me.

He and I talked about the problem and he told me no one understood the covenants and didn't want to comply with them. When I asked him what he was telling the residents, he said he told them to keep things clean or they had to pay on time, etc. Invariably, though, conversations turned into a yelling match. I told the manager to carry the covenants with him at all times and when he approached someone, show them the paragraph with which they weren't complying and explain it; always maintaining a level tone of voice. When he started reading the covenants and explaining what they meant, the residents started doing what they were required to do and the complaints stopped. When the manager's communication became clear and concise, the residents understood and most complied. If someone is not in compliance with the covenants, don't always expect them to understand what they need to do without a calm explanation.

The information you provide to a customer needs to be thorough. Don't hide anything from them—get everything out in the open. Give them the bad with the good if the situation calls for it. You don't want a customer to tell you, "You didn't tell me I'd get an eviction notice!" or anything similar. There should be no surprises for the customer.

Make More Effort Than Is Expected. You know—go the extra mile. Your customers count on you. Exceed a customer's expectations and you will have them as a customer for a long time. Do a little bit extra to satisfy your customers. A contented customer is one less problem you will have. Contented customers tell their friends you can be trusted so they are great referrals.

The best customer is the one you already have. Be a Compassionate Cheerleader.

CUSTOMER SERVICE MADE SIMPLE

> Be happy, be thankful, look for the good in all,
> care deeply, try hard, stay upbeat,
> be knowledgeable, listen, enjoy life and
>
> **SMILE!**

HIRE THE ATTITUDE

I think everyone in the service business should have the attitude of a Compassionate Cheerleader. Those are the type of people I have tried to hire over the years. If I don't hear or see a smile during the first two sentences in my first conversation with a prospective employee, I don't waste any more of my time with them.

Of course, someone who isn't smiling may be the most qualified person and may be the best in carrying out the policies and procedures put in place. Others may be happy with a non-smiler because they can provide what is needed to run the business.

But I am not satisfied. These people have to interact with customers and a naturally happy person is going to make a much better impression on them than someone who doesn't appear happy. I have found people who do not automatically smile don't always handle customers' problems with a calm, helpful demeanor and often fake a more appropriate attitude than the negative one that comes more naturally to them. And believe me, **your customers can see through insincerity.**

You can teach skills, but you can't teach ATTITUDE.

Don't be afraid of terminating someone from their position in order to hire the right person. Putting off the inevitable only hurts you in the long run. Every mistake, every project that isn't finished and every unhappy customer is costing the business. If the job description for the position has been carefully explained and given in written form to the person you are hiring, they are ultimately responsible for being true to themselves and to you about being able to fulfill their duties. If they cannot, you must move on.

This is not to say I have fired everyone who couldn't immediately do their job. I haven't. Years ago, a manager was hired for a large multi-family community. She had a fantastic attitude and great rapport with the residents. Customer service was definitely one of her strengths. She could hardly come up with the correct answer to 2+2, though. Forget figuring out a percentage of anything. Keeping track of monthly expenditures to compare to the budget was very difficult for her. She and I had lesson after lesson after lesson when she needed to work with numbers. She never gave up, didn't let it affect her attitude, and little by little improved.

After about two years, she flew into my office one day with a big smile on her face, waving some paper in the air. She exclaimed she had finally completed a particular financial report all by herself. It was a joyous day for her and for me too. It took two years, but she was now on her way to being an all-around great manager.

You have to care enough to train people well. It takes time and patience you may not have or may not want to expend. But in the end, it is so worth it. This manager with a great attitude was good at many things and the residents would do anything she asked. She blossomed into the real deal with some help. I didn't have to teach her attitude—only skills.

There is very little difference in people, but that little difference makes a big difference. The little difference is attitude.

The big difference is whether it is positive or negative.

—Clement Stone

CHAPTER 5
STREAMLINING OPERATIONS TO MAXIMIZE RETURN

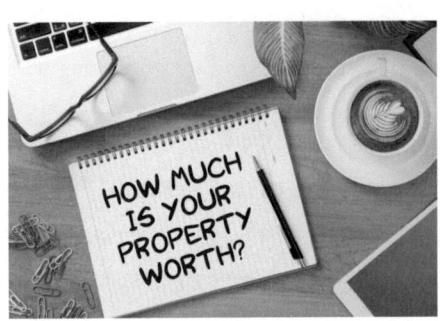

A major function of a real estate asset manager is to streamline operations and maximize the return on investment for the client. If you aren't doing this, then please read this carefully. The client doesn't need you if you don't know how.

A real estate investor invests his money to make money. The *Merriam-Webster Dictionary*'s definition of invest is "to commit (money) in order to earn a financial return." It's pretty simple then. When you manage real estate, the assets are expected to achieve a profit, usually the more the better.

If you are working with a client who hasn't invested in an asset to make a profit, then you may want to run away—fast! Because something you don't want to know about or be a part of is probably going on. In my younger years, it took me two weeks to figure out the business owner I was working for opened his office as a front for selling illegal drugs. Yes, I was naïve and a bit slow on the uptake. A few years ago, I met with a real estate investor who talked a big game. I came away from the conversation with the opinion that he hired managers at what was barely minimum wage and treated them like puppets on a string. Something felt wrong to me. Later, I read he was convicted of tax evasion. I guess you could say he had invested to make a profit, however, I don't think money he had in his possession by not paying taxes would really be considered "profit."

How do you achieve the highest possible profit? You **streamline operations** to reduce expenses and increase revenue. To take our English lesson a bit further, the definition of streamline is to "alter in order to make more efficient or simple." Thus, you take away everything that is not essential to operations, then you organize and simplify what is left. In a nutshell, you make operations faster and such that they can be completed with less effort.

Fast and simple isn't all that hard to do and it sure makes overall management less intensive. So why do most people who have never done it before shy away from streamlining? Because they think "I've always done it this way" is easier than changing anything and what they are doing now has pretty much worked for them. Well, change is needed because the operations of many assets can still be streamlined and a higher return on investment realized.

To prove this point, I'll tell you the story of what happened after I acquired the management of two apartment home communities purchased by a client. Both communities were fairly new developments and both were considered to be among the best in town. They suffered from low occupancy and negative cash flow, however.

I went to work on these two communities and this is what was accomplished. We:

- Reorganized and revitalized operations,

- Lowered market rents—yes, lowered them because they were so high the communities were not competing in the marketplace,

- Recruited new staff,

- Slashed expenses, and

- Realigned advertising and marketing.

These are the results of the two communities combined after just **four months**:

- Occupancy increased from 78% to 94%, a 16% increase,

- Annualized revenues increased $700,000, and

- Value of the properties increased $8,250,000

See why knowing how to streamline operations and maximize resources is so important?

ARE THE RIGHT PEOPLE ON BOARD?

One of the first things I do when I acquire a management account is assess the personnel, if there are personnel for that specific property. This is because we always need to make sure the right people are on board and they are fulfilling their responsibilities.

People are the most important asset of a company. They are the ones who represent ownership and management and they are the ambassadors for the client's asset. They will see that the practices for streamlining operations and maximizing returns are implemented and managed.

I often find properties are overstaffed. I assume the owner or management company thinks if more people are hired, the work will get done. When it doesn't, another person is hired. What really needs to happen is to make sure staff is being managed well, every person is doing the job they need to do, and all are held accountable for the results. Throwing more people at a problem isn't the solution.

In my opinion, personnel is one of the most time-consuming components of management. So when you add more people, you add more personalities, more personal issues, more paperwork, more paychecks, more payroll costs, more risk, and more heads to oversee. This decreases efficiency; it doesn't increase it. Having the leanest staff possible is always my ultimate goal. That means you have to have good people—the right people.

This is what I assess for each person on staff:

- Does he have a positive attitude?

- Does he have initiative and take action?

- Is he a decision maker?

- Does he work smart?

- Does he have a desire to learn new skills, if necessary?

- Is he willing to support the practices put in place?

I watch, I listen, I train, I assist, I provide support and all the while, I assess. The team is working well when things like this happen:

1. A manager asked me if I would show him how to read a financial statement so he would know if his efforts to decrease expenses and increase revenue were improving the financial condition of his property. He wasn't afraid to tell me this was something he had never learned. He wanted to learn it in order to do his job better. He moved on to overseeing other properties.

2. A manager's attitude was **whatever it takes**, I'll do. He kept the smile on his face and put forth the effort to do what it took. He eventually became a Regional Director for another management company.

3. Without hesitation, a department manager at a hospitality property took over the management of the maintenance department because the position was vacated without notice and he did a fabulous job.

4. The maintenance tech says "I'll handle it"—and does. There is no time spent complaining and no need for continual check-ups on a job that is taking forever.

5. The manager says, "I became swimming pool certified so I could figure out why Dan was spending so much time maintaining the pool and supplies were costing more."

6. The leasing agent says, "I just did a market survey and we need to consider increasing rental rates."

7. A tenant compliments the Facilities Manager on a speedy repair.

8. The pro shop attendant says, "You don't need to hire anyone else—I can handle those shifts by myself."

The team isn't working so well when:

1. The office assistant says, "That job is not in my job description."

2. The manager is too busy to see that a delinquent account is collected.

3. The maintenance tech is rude to a resident.

4. When one of the staff says, "That's a stupid policy so I am not following it."

5. When an assistant manager says, "My job is to kick people out of here and if you aren't going to let me, then I'm leaving." I'd never heard that one before. Didn't know that was why were in this business. I decided this was one guy I didn't want to learn anything from.

6. A manager told me he thought he had things under control and we were on the same page now, and I had to break it to him we weren't even on the same planet yet.

Thus, there will be times when a change is necessary. A machine needs all its parts in working order to run well. When one is broken beyond repair, it simply needs to be replaced. Same with the people who are expected to be members of a good, efficient team.

A staff is usually only as good as the person leading them. Keep this in mind when assessing personnel and yourself.

During my initial visit to an asset I acquired, I watched a guy on a riding mower mow grass all week long. I saw the same thing on the next visit. He drove that mower slower than molasses and it was what he did all day long, five days a week. Back and forth, back and forth, sometimes over the same areas he did the day before.

I asked the Community Manager about him. This is how the conversation went:

> Me: "He is really slow. How long does it take him to mow the entire property?"
>
> Manager: "He gets it all done in a week."
>
> Me: "But if it takes that long, when does he have time to do anything else?"

Manager: "He doesn't know how to do anything else. He was hired to mow, so that is all he does. He is really good at it, too."

Me: "Why does it take him so long and why does he mow some areas twice? So he can get his forty hours in?"

Manager: "Oh, no. He wants the grass to look good."

That ridiculousness stopped. The guy was asked to get the mowing done in a timelier manner so he could perform other minor maintenance jobs. He got the mowing done more quickly, but he never pulled his weight on any other job he was given, no matter how simple it was. The reason he gave was that riding a lawn mower is easy and he didn't like to work hard. We tried.

He was replaced with someone who got the mowing done in two to three days and then spent the rest of the time performing other maintenance work. Result: One less person to pay. Efficient. Simple.

And you know what else? The manager didn't like the new way the asset was being managed. So she quit. A manager that allows team members to do only what they want instead of what is best for the client is not someone who should be in real estate management. If she didn't want to make changes to what wasn't working, she would soon be gone—even if it wasn't her decision.

This situation is not unusual. A lender hired an asset management company I worked with to take over the management of a multi-family property acquired through foreclosure. In most situations, I think it best to retain existing personnel in a property where ownership or management has changed. They are the ones who have formed relationships with residents or tenants and who know the property and operations best. Therefore, all personnel remained at this particular community…in the beginning.

This property had an Old West theme. In the West, in cowboy country, this sounds like a really cool theme for a property. However, a dilapidated Old West theme isn't so cool. When the property was built, old stagecoach wheels, wagons, and farm implements were positioned in the common areas. Through the years, the themed objects remained in place. They were not maintained and the grass was allowed to grow under and around them. (Ever heard of a weed eater?) Eventually, the common areas looked like they hadn't been maintained since the days of the Old West. This was the condition when the lender took possession. Deferred maintenance was found in other areas as well.

Residents were moving out and there weren't new residents to take their place. It's difficult to attract new quality residents when a property doesn't look nice. The first thing we did was decide to get rid of the theme and remove the Old West objects. Then we began cleaning up the common areas. The General Manager wanted no part of the change and left immediately. The Community Manager stuck around for a couple of weeks. Then she too left because we were changing something she had been a part of and loved, and because she felt I was rude.

I am not rude. If I was, I would have probably said something like, "The lender is in charge now. So how has the Old West worked for you so far?" But I didn't. Instead I said: "I don't want you leave. I want you to support the changes we are making, but if you can't, then I understand you need to leave."

To be the best in this business, you work to meet or exceed an investor's goals. The job isn't all about you. Every once in a while, someone is going to have an idea that is better than yours. You must see that a property is maintained at a high-quality level and that cash flow is at its maximum. You can't sit back and think, "This is how it's always been done." Markets change, resident and tenant profiles change, investors' goals change, and facilities get older. Keep an open mind, learn from others, and adapt to change.

This Old West situation is a good example of property management vs. asset management. The managers cared only for managing the property and its Old West theme. They didn't understand the financial problems being experienced by the investor. If they did, perhaps they would have made appropriate changes and the lender would not have become the owner.

Instead, new management for the community was hired, deferred maintenance decreased, the property was maintained at a higher level, and new residents were attracted to the community and moved in. The result was the lender now had a viable asset to sell. It all started with the right people in place who had a "can do" attitude and who could implement the turnaround plan and see it through.

I've walked into management offices only to see someone sitting there reading a book or engrossed in a personal phone call. I've found employees coming in late every day or taking a longer break or lunch than allowed. We don't pay people to relax. We pay people to work when they are supposed to be working. Perhaps an extra person is needed for the busy hours. Assess whether the position can be changed to part time to cover those hours instead of paying someone to work all day when it isn't really needed. Or give the person more responsibility, even in other departments, so they work full time but fill two part-time positions.

I told you in the Introduction that this book was very personal. I am going to take a time out here and get a bit personal so you can better understand why I say what I say and take the actions I take.

My father no longer has much of a memory, but he still remembers I want to clean anything that is dirty and that I have a hard time seeing somebody hurt. When he told me this recently, I thought about it a lot. Self-reflection, I guess. I want to help those who are hurt or struggling, I don't watch movies or television shows where someone gets hurt, and blood and injury bothers me because someone is sick or hurt. Is it any wonder I gave up going into the medical field?

I think this is why it is difficult for me to deal with personnel when things aren't working out. I am going to hurt them with my actions. So I have learned to handle it in my own way.

There are two events from my very early career that changed the way I work with personnel.

The company I worked with had a property with two husband and wife teams; one couple served as managers of the property and the other as assistant managers. This was more common years ago than it is today. Management of the property was not good and it was decided with the owner that both couples would be relieved of their duties. This was my first experience in letting someone go.

My associate and I told the manager couple and they left without incident. We told the assistant manager couple and they both started crying and saying they only did what the managers told them. We both felt sorry for them and wanted to give them another chance.

I called the owner and told him we thought we should keep the assistant manager couple. He told me we all knew they were not going to be able to do the job and I needed to toughen up, proceed as planned, and move on. I knew he was right so I toughened up and tried not to think about this couple who now had no job and nowhere to go.

The second event concerned a very dear friend of mine. My husband and I became very good friends with this Community Manager and her husband, such good friends that we asked them to be godparents to our younger son. She got into some personal trouble no one knew about and did something at work she should have never done. I wanted to help her out of her situation, but I had to fire her instead. The transgression was so serious, I had no choice. Talk about having to toughen up! I had to fire my friend and the godmother of my child.

So early on, I got tough. I couldn't cry, I couldn't feel, and I couldn't help. So to keep my sanity, I no longer formed personal relationships with those I managed. (Most people already know this, but I learned the hard way.) Since then I've had many great working relationships—they just aren't on a close personal level. My personal life and my work life became two different lives for me.

I've trained and worked with someone as long as I can to try to remedy a problem. But when the time came that a change had to be made in the best interests of the client, I made it. I have and will always remain loyal to the needs of my clients and to those I work for. It's not that I don't care—I do. But I have a job to do and I do it.

I don't care what anyone says, if you have compassion for others, it is going to be difficult to deal with these types of issues. You have to deal with them though. How you do it has to be your personal decision. I've told you how I deal with it, but that doesn't make it the right way. Some would say my way isn't the right way because it is so hardhearted. I don't know how else to do it. I have to hurt people and I can't dwell on it so I don't.

Those who are employed should work to their potential. If they can't do the job, they should be true to themselves and to the person hiring them and not take the job in the first place. For those of you out there who are employed and struggling, ask for help, study, and learn something new. Try. Grow yourself.

Never be unemployed and never be triflingly employed.

—*John Wesley*

It is difficult to streamline operations without the right people in place. Thus for me, the assessment of personnel comes first. The right people with training, credentials, skills, and experience may cost more than others. The wages and salaries of specific positions, therefore, are not necessarily reduced when you make changes. But when you have the right people who have a positive attitude and the appropriate knowledge, you can create efficiencies in operations.

If you are in charge, whether a real estate manager or investor who self-manages, and you don't know how to streamline operations, then you need to learn how to, learn to live with mediocrity, or get out of the business. I chose to learn because I wanted to be the best. What is your choice?

MAXIMIZE EFFICIENCY AND ELIMINATE UNNECESSARY COSTS

While you are putting the right people in place, you will want to consider how they can maximize efficiency in operations and eliminate unnecessary costs. When you do this, you will have a better idea of the staff required. Will you cut positions or add positions?

Some of the things you will be analyzing and determining may include the following:

1. Does it make cost saving and/or efficiency sense to contract out work done currently by staff?, or

2. Vice versa, does it make sense to have current or additional staff do work currently contracted out?, or

3. If a contractor has been hired because his professional license is required, will he permit staff to perform some of the day-to-day work with his oversight to reduce the cost of the contracted work?

Examples of the type of work mentioned above are landscaping and turf maintenance, swimming pool maintenance, building maintenance, janitorial work, electrical and plumbing work, heavy equipment operation, equipment maintenance, IT/computer repair, and marketing.

A hospitality property experienced cost savings, improved results, and higher guest satisfaction when staff was hired to perform janitorial services, replacing a contractor.

In a multi-family property, cost savings were realized when staff was replaced with a contractor to perform landscaping and turf maintenance.

You need to make detailed analyses of expenses. The results for each expense are not the same for every property. Where hiring a contractor may save money for one, it may not for another property.

When you are comparing costs of an employee versus a contractor, don't forget to add employment taxes, benefits, and worker's compensation insurance to the cost of hiring someone.

You want to determine, too, whether upgrading technology systems will reduce staff, reduce costs, increase efficiencies, and/or increase customer satisfaction.

1. If you haven't already, consider using **internet-based management software**. It can create efficiencies and reduce costs. You pay for only the services you need, it reduces the amount of IT support needed, staff can work from anywhere, work is updated in real time for all to see and share, and productivity is increased with less hours worked by staff.

2. Consider using a **screening service** if decisions on prospective resident applications are still being made by individuals. Less time will be spent reviewing background reports and making the decision. Also, having a decision made by a service reduces a property's risk of non-compliance with fair housing laws.

3. To streamline posting payments to individual account, purchase **check scanners** that work with the management software so checks, cashier's checks, and money orders can be scanned and electronically entered into the software. Some software will automatically transfer the deposits to your bank, eliminating time to drive deposits to the bank.

4. Electronic payment solutions create efficiencies, reduce costs, and decrease delinquent payments. Customers find ACH, credit card and 24/7 online payments convenient. And there are no checks to post. If you accept credit cards

you should find out if you must comply with the Payment Card Industry Data Security Standards (PCI) and train staff on an annual basis.

ANALYZE EXPENSES

Expense line items need to be analyzed. Some of the things you will be thinking about and determining will include the following:

- Are there services that can be eliminated or decreased?

- Have I anticipated all ongoing maintenance requirements?

- Are certain expenses increasing and by how much?

- Should any expenses be passed through to residents or tenants?

- Do expenses seem reasonable and/or in line with industry standards?

Knowing if an expense looks correct is much simpler if you know about how much the expense should be in the first place. One day when meeting with a prospective client, it took only a quick glance at his income and expense statement to find an expense that appeared to be too high. It turned out that his current management company was charging contractors a kickback fee. The kickback was hidden in the invoices and paid to the contractors, thus increasing the expense. The contractor in turn paid the money to the management company. This was certainly not ethical and it definitely didn't maximize the client's return. The client fired his management company and hired our company.

Investors, beware! There are management companies that increase expenses to pay themselves. I recently spoke to a client of a vacation home management company. The management company is adding fees from ten percent to forty percent to utility and contractor invoices. The company fired one of its contractors because he wouldn't increase his invoiced rate to pay off the management company. The client's account has been charged these expenses but she was not made aware of the upcharge for the management company or the reason her chosen contractor was fired. The fee and commission for managing this vacation home are low in my estimation. The management company found a way to make more money by padding invoices. The problem is, they did it secretively, which simply is not right.

When a management company submits a proposal, make sure the proposal includes the management fee and that any additional fees are disclosed. There should be no hidden fees that will surprise you later. Generally, managers who have a real estate license or are members of a trade association are bound by ethics codes. You may want to ask management companies what licenses or certifications they have.

If you aren't familiar enough with standard expenses or want to make sure the expenses at your property are in line with other similar properties, benchmarking reports are offered by some industry associations such as:

1. Institute of Real Estate Management—Apartments, office buildings, shopping centers, condominiums, cooperatives, and Planned Unit Developments (PUDs)

2. Building Owners and Management Association—Commercial Properties

3. National Apartment Association

4. American Hotel and Lodging Association

Check with other associations you may be familiar with to see if they have information you can use for comparative purposes.

I will provide you with some basic expense items to check. I can't list all of them because I don't know your property. I hope this gets you started, though.

- Make sure only the items needed and a reasonable stock of those items are purchased. These things should be stored in a neat and organized way so they can be easily found by staff and easily inventoried. I've asked a facilities manager if there is anything he needs to do his job better and been told he didn't have enough supplies in stock to perform ordinary maintenance on a daily basis. All this while standing in a shop in complete disarray. How did he know the supplies weren't there? Once he organized the storage, he found that he had plenty of what he needed and it was now accessible.

- Make sure all equipment is serviced properly. Repairs due to negligence are more expensive than preventative maintenance.

- Bid out replacement appliances and heating and cooling equipment to see if the property could pay less with another vendor. I called the manufacturer of rooftop air conditioning units for a very large apartment property and asked if we could purchase units directly from them to save money. That practice was not permitted, but they gave me the name of a handful of preferred dealers in the metropolitan area. One was happy to have the business. Instead of continuing to use the current contractor, the property saved over $1,000 per unit by using a preferred dealer who made a deal with us to get the business.

- If you have contracts for lawn and landscape maintenance, janitorial, pest control, security, etc., bid the work out initially and then every two or three years again to make sure the property isn't paying too much.

- See that appropriate safety equipment and safety policies are in place and there are no slip and fall obstacles on the property. There could be cost savings in insurance with fewer injuries.

- Analyze utility usage and rates to make sure the property is not overusing or overpaying. Make sure you are aware of any upcoming utility rate increases. During an audit of the water bill for a large apartment community, I discovered the capital improvement charge had been overcharged by the municipality. I contacted the water department on numerous occasions about the discrepancy, however, they refused to fix the situation in the end. I then went to city government and successfully negotiated the recalculation of the charges. The community received a $15,000 refund and the new calculation of ongoing charges resulted in ongoing savings of $15,000 per year.

- Order office supplies online and have delivered to the site instead of staff traveling to a store.

- Have companies provide proposals to bundle phone and internet to reduce costs.

- Make sure the property tax assessor's office has the correct information from which to value the property for real estate taxes. If based on valuation, how does the property compare to comparable properties? If based on income, does the assessor's office have current financial information? Determine whether a service should be hired to appeal valuations.
One year I delivered the most recent annual income and expense statement for a property to the assessor's office and the assessor lowered the valuation, saving thousands in property taxes. Don't expect it to always be that simple though. Sometimes it becomes a real fight.

- Make sure coverage is in place for property and liability insurance. Also, confirm that the values of properties are correct. Lowering values that have automatically increased to an amount too high, raising deductibles, or eliminating unnecessary coverage can reduce insurance costs.

ANALYZE REVENUE

You want to make sure a property is generating the maximum revenue possible.

The bulk of the revenue comes from the rent charged. Unless your lease requires a different parameter for setting rents, the main guideline to follow to determine what the market rental rate(s) will be is to charge what the market will bear—or what a resident or tenant is willing to pay.

This means you need to know the market at all times. You may be told to do a market survey annually, but I don't think this is often enough. I think twice a year should be the minimum. I don't think you need to play games and pretend you are a customer or any other person when you call or visit a competitor. I have found that you learn more when you are truthful about who you are and the purpose of your inquiry.

You don't need a formal market survey to know the market. If the property manager listens to prospects, he will always know what competitors are charging because prospects will tell him. Other managers, real estate brokers, contractors, vendors, etc., are a wealth of information and usually happy to share what they know about the market. You should also read the local real estate news to keep up to date on the market.

When you know the market, you can make market rental increases accordingly, or decreases in a slow rental market. Market rent is what you will be charging a new resident or tenant and it can change at any time, depending on the market. If you have maintained the property at a quality level, you should be able to charge the same or similar rent as your competitors. If your property is superior and has excellent management, then you may be able to charge a higher rent. In areas that are not rent-controlled (which is most of the country), you can charge as high a rent as you want as long as prospects are willing to pay it and move in. If the rent is too high, however, and no one is willing to pay the market rent, then you will sit on vacancies and that doesn't make anyone any money.

For existing residents and tenants, you may not charge more than the rent specified in a current lease until the lease expires. Once a lease expires, you don't necessarily have to increase the rent to market rate. You may choose to offer smaller increases to existing residents and tenants so they will stay. Be fair and treat everyone alike to reduce fair housing issues. You might set a fixed amount to increase all renewing residents or tenants. Or determine a rental rate to which you want everyone increased regardless of their current rent. Don't ever increase rent in a discriminatory manner or in retaliation.

Don't shy away from increasing rent because you are afraid that residents or tenants will move. If they are being treated as they want to be treated, they probably won't be going anywhere. You should regularly increase rent, no matter how small the increase, so it isn't a shock to the resident or tenant and to maximize the revenue for the property. If you don't regularly increase rent and then implement a large increase all at once, it is a bigger shock and the resident or tenant may be more likely to move.

Owning income property is a business, so you should not be afraid to increase rents. Revenue is what pays the expenses and pays you. You should charge as much rent as the market will bear. On the other hand, the business needs to be competitive, so make a good, informed decision when setting the rates.

You should also review fees such as application fees and washer/dryer rates and determine if an increase is in order.

Determine if any ancillary services can be added to increase revenue or if some services need to be eliminated or replaced if they are not generating enough revenue. Some services to consider may be:

- Telecom agreements

- Vacuum cleaner rental

- Pet deposits

- Key deposits

- Rooftop agreements with communications companies

- Advertising in the property's newsletter

- Resident renter's insurance

- Business referral fees

- Vending machine revenue

- Wi-Fi services

- Valet trash service

- Dry cleaning pickup and delivery

- Recreational equipment rentals

- Storage rental

- Food or grocery delivery

- Snack bar or food truck

Be knowledgeable about what services are important to your residents and the market. Remember too, they may be turned off by too many choices or too many extra fees added to their rent. A service may be more satisfactory to residents if it is included in a slightly higher rent. Know your residents and you will make better decisions.

Now you have made sure the right people are on board, streamlined the operations, reviewed and reduced expenses, and reviewed and increased revenue. The investors' return has been maximized and the value of the property hopefully increased. Don't get complacent, though, as making sure a property is positioned correctly is an ongoing process.

MANAGEMENT MAKEOVER

CHAPTER 6
UNDERSTANDING YOUR NUMBERS

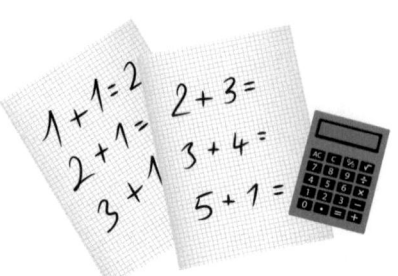

We know unnecessary costs need to be cut from operations. We know expenses should be reduced when possible. We know we should take full advantage of additional income streams and increased rents and fees to increase revenue. But if you aren't performing these tasks correctly in the first place, the income potential of a property will not be at its maximum.

My three largest pet peeves in this area of management are things that if not done correctly will inhibit the financial success of a property. I see manager after manager stumbling their way through and I always wonder: Where has common sense gone? And yet, most are not even aware there is a problem.

There may be no perceivable problems. Things are running smoothly. Work is getting done. Bills are being paid. The owner makes a profit every month. If you don't know what you are doing wrong, then how do you know there is a problem?

Read through the rest of this chapter. If there is just one little tiny thing that applies to you or to your manager, then there could be a problem. You may not find out how costly the problem is until someone does it right and more dollars flow to the bottom line. That will be the scorecard to let you know you had a problem.

The three things to which I think all managers should be attentive are:

- Carefully crafting budgets and forecasts, meeting the investor's financial goals and objectives to the best of your ability;

- Making sound decisions when purchasing goods or services; and

- Justifying all expenditures.

IT'S ALL IN THE BUDGET

Dictionary.com defines budget, in part, as:

1. an estimate, often itemized, of expected income and expense for a given period in the future.

2. a plan of operations based on such an estimate.

You know what your current revenue is. You figure in rent increases and any expected increase in occupancy. You compile historical data of expenses, talk to vendors and contractors about future costs, and find out what increases in utilities, taxes, etc., there may be. Then you input the estimates of expected income and expenses into budget format just like you learned. And, hurrah! You have a budget.

But often there is more to it than that. A budget requires meaningful research and attention to detail. You need to be aware of what the owner's ultimate goals are for the budgeted period. Determining the goals of the asset first will provide you the information necessary to prepare the budget with the necessary revenue and expenditures to meet those goals. A budget provides the planning tool to be proactive in meeting the goals of the owner.

You should revisit advertising and marketing based upon your plans for occupancy and retention. You should continue to look for ways to create efficiencies and study the most recent market trends. The budget should include services, necessary maintenance, and capital improvements and reserves that will maintain and enhance the value of the property. Change is constant and you need to plan for it and adapt operations accordingly.

When created and used properly, a budget gives you guidelines for the operation of an asset. When an owner receives the budget, they expect the property to perform according to that budget. Sure, there will be items over or under budget. It is your job to manage the budget. If one line item is over budget, you should try to make it up on another line item, by seeing that it is under budget. The goal is to plan how to operate the asset according to the budget so the goals of the owner are met and the owner has the amount of cash flow indicated on the budget (or much more) at year end.

I worked with a client who had promised a specific annual return to the investors of one of the assets we managed for him. I created what I thought was a realistic draft budget and gave it to him. Problem was it wasn't realistic to the client because the budgeted cash flow wasn't enough to disburse to the investors. My directive was to create a budget that provided sufficient cash flow for disbursements.

This meant revenue had to increase and expenses had to decrease. And I had to do this at a time when the economy was terrible and the rental market was soft. Remember I asked earlier if you stay in your safe, tidy little world without thinking outside the box? Well, this was when I learned to think outside the box. And the client helped me learn this lesson.

I agonized over this budget. I took out wage and salary increases because how could I justify payroll increases when the revenue was continually decreasing? But I did work in bonuses if we met budget at year end. I slashed expenses until I knew the property could not be maintained well if I slashed any more. And still I didn't come up with sufficient cash flow to pay the investors.

I went back to the revenue side to determine where increases could be made. This was a large apartment community with eighty percent occupancy. Two months free rent with a ninety-nine dollar security deposit was being offered to new move-ins. In a good market, occupancy stayed at ninety-nine percent every month with no incentives. I knew we could hit the numbers if twenty more apartment homes were rented. (There were almost fifty vacancies.)

I added a few more dollars to the advertising budget, and proposed six months free rent—the most I had ever seen before in this particular market—and added rent for twenty more apartment homes in the budget. Thank goodness! The numbers worked.

I sent it back to the client. His response? He didn't think six months free rent was enough to rent twenty apartment homes so he wanted to increase free rent to one year. No one did that!

I could see two problems right away.

1. Leasing apartments without rent for a year does not increase revenue for the coming year.

2. If someone doesn't have a rent payment for a year, they may not plan well enough to have the money to start paying market rent the thirteenth month.

Was this impossible to do?

Nothing is impossible to a willing heart!

—John Heywood

I thought if we could rent twenty apartment homes at six months free rent, then we could rent forty at one year free rent. But instead of giving one year up front, we'd discount rent fifty percent for two years. I added forty apartment homes at half rent to the budget and the numbers still worked.

And that is exactly what happened. Just over forty apartment homes were rented in less than two months. Right on time to have the rent coming in at the beginning of the year when the budgeted period began.

No competitor was offering what amounted to a year of free rent. If this property didn't attract everyone in the market for an apartment home, it attracted most of them for the next two months. In lean times there usually aren't enough renters to fill every apartment building. As this story shows, there are ways to attract more than your share. You can attract every potential customer if you really want to.

We knew two things going into this program: 1) Half rent doesn't get you as good a resident as one who pays full rent, and 2) The market is cyclical, so we were hoping two years would be enough for things to turn around. It so happened, two years was sufficient.

During the two years of the program, we lost four of the residents who were paying half rent—either because they didn't want to follow the guidelines and regulations of the community or because they didn't pay the monthly rent. At the end of the two years, half of the more than forty residents on the program stayed and began paying market rent. The program was successful. The community generated the revenue needed to fund disbursements in a slow market and it ended up with over twenty really good residents. The best resident is the one you already have!

I learned four things from creating a budget for this apartment community:

1. A budget is important. It is what a client uses to plan financially for the budget period.

2. It's all in the dollars. Play with them until you figure it out.

3. Why settle for your share of the market when you can have it all!

4. A community can still thrive on a lean expense budget. I did not increase expenditures after the two-year program, except for typical increases in costs of items such as payroll, materials, contractor rates, and utilities. Every other asset I've managed has had a lean expense budget as well. Streamlining operations is easy if you put your mind to it—and you get the staff on board.

Budgets should be realistic. Sure, you can plan operations to increase occupancy and rental rates and decrease some expenses. In fact, that usually isn't a bad plan. However, budgeting revenue that depends on absolute one hundred percent occupancy with two hundred dollar per month rent increases across the board in a multi-family property probably isn't realistic. (Don't roll your eyes. It has happened.) It is pretty much guaranteed there will be move-outs that will require at least a few days of down time to make the units market ready. Considering only that one factor, the revenue budgeted for this property could not be met. It would be great if there was no turnover and every resident began paying two hundred dollars per month more upon renewal. The owner probably loved that budget. Why try to fool everyone for the short term though? It isn't realistic.

Budgets are also a means by which to pay bonuses to staff. Usually they have to meet or exceed various budget lines in order to receive a bonus. You want to make sure the goal for the bonus is a goal you actually want the property to meet. Again, your expectations should be realistic. Handing unrealistic budget goals to staff members doesn't make them work harder—they give up before they even start.

Pay attention to the budgets you create. Understand monthly variances so adjustments can be made before the community is so far over budget it can't be reined in. Report variances so everyone involved understands the property's financial position. Know when to recommend a budget revision if circumstances warrant a revision.

A budget is your roadmap for the coming budgeted period. It should be used and checked continually. If I ask a manager to see the budget and it is pulled from a file without dog-eared edges, coffee stains, pencil markings, and the like, I become a bit suspicious of management performance. Budgets are made for a reason. The owner expects the budget to be met and it is the owner's goals you are attempting to achieve.

COMPARE APPLES TO APPLES—NOT APPLES TO ORANGES

I have come to the conclusion there are managers who have learned they must obtain bids for certain projects and services, but they were never taught how to compare the bids to make an informed decision.

I am beginning to think the most common process by which many real estate managers obtain bids is to call a number of contractors, briefly tell them what the work is, and hope they all include the same job duties and responsibilities in their bid. Hoping isn't going to get you very far, especially when no two contractors normally look at the job the same way without some direction.

Managers, you have to compare bids to make a recommendation. Not just look at the total cost and recommend the lowest one.

I sat on the board of an association that requested the manager find a contractor to service building equipment that had not been serviced in years. So we could choose a contractor, the manager submitted two bids to us and recommended we choose the lower one. One was almost three hundred dollars and the other about five hundred dollars. While everyone at the table was agreeing with him, I glanced at the bids. The differences were so apparent they stood out like flashing neon lights. I was the only one who saw those lights, however.

The lower bid included cleaning and oiling the equipment one time. The higher bid included cleaning and oiling the equipment, checking the Freon, and replacing filters three times during the year. When the differences were pointed out, the board decided the higher bid was the best, particularly when filters need to be changed more than once a year.

The good thing about the two bids was that the work to be done was itemized by both contractors. Make sure you ask that all work be itemized on bids submitted to you. Otherwise, how can you compare what is being done and how much each of the items will cost? This also makes it easier to eliminate single items for cost savings because you know the cost of each in an itemized bid.

The difficulty presented by the two bids in this case was that the job duties and responsibilities were not the same. We could not compare costs for "apples to apples" work. Because this was a small job and we wanted to get it done, we simply made a decision on the information presented. If it had been a larger job, we would have asked for new bids so we could make a more informed decision.

You need proper and complete information in order to make sound decisions. Luckily, I was involved in a large project during my early career that included an engineer's sealed bid process. I was able to review the invitation to bid, along with specifications and drawings before they were provided to the contractors. I saw how it was done and learned the only way for contractors to bid "apples to apples" is to give them the specifications of the project and make those specifications part of the bid and then the contract. I have carried that knowledge with me through the years.

When asking for a bid, the scope of work needs to be given to the contractor, no matter how small the project. You won't always have an engineer completing the drawings and specs, so if you don't know what the scope of work should be, then educate yourself. You can find out how to do almost anything on the internet these days. Meet with contractors and ask them for their opinions. Involve a professional or someone on your team that understands the project and get their recommendations. In the end, the contractors working on a proposal should all have the same specifications. And if you receive a bid with additional work and you want to include it, have the other contractors add it to their bid.

I worked with a young manager who was having a small asphalt overlay project bid. Instead of providing the contractors with a written scope of work, she told them verbally. When I reviewed the bids, two were for sealing the asphalt and two were for overlaying the asphalt. When I asked the manager why, she asked me if there was a difference in the two applications. See how easy it is for contractors to bid the wrong thing? If you don't know the terminology, then learn it. If you have written specs, then use them.

Another thing to look out for when comparing bids is whether the contractor has bid time and materials or has provided a fixed price. A fixed price is the amount that will be paid to the contractor for the scope of work to be done. On a time and materials basis, the cost could be lower or higher, depending on how long the job takes or on the cost and amount of materials used.

I often like a time and materials bid because the cost of the project can actually be less than forecasted. But I always ask the contractor for a "not to exceed" bid so there are no cost surprises at the end. This means that the contractor will submit a bid for actual time and materials, however, there is a maximum that will be charged even if actual costs are higher. Having a maximum cost will better enable you to compare the fixed price bids to the time and materials bid as well.

When you are managing real estate, it is your responsibility to understand what needs to be done and make sound decisions. It is your responsibility to spend an owner's money wisely. If you are making recommendations or decisions based on bids that are not comparable, then those are not sound recommendations or decisions based on proper information.

Provide the scope of work to those bidding a project and then compare bids line by line to make sure each is bidding the same work and it is the scope of work you have created and are expecting.

DON'T JUST BE A CHECK SIGNER

I was walking down the hall to my office one day and saw a client sitting at the desk of one of our real estate managers. Seemed a bit odd to me. I walked in the office and asked her what she was doing. She had questions about what was being paid to the landscape contractor for her property because she thought it was too much. When she asked the real estate manager about the invoices, he told her she could use his office to go through the invoices. *What?*

I immediately told the client it was our job to review invoices and to be able to tell her, the client, what was being spent and why. I told her she could feel free to leave the research to me and I would send the information to her. I basically kicked her out of the office, but in this situation, she wasn't at all unhappy about it.

By the way, the manager was terminated from his position. You do not retain clients by letting them do the work. That is why you were hired in the first place.

What I found in the landscape company's invoices is that they were charging for materials and labor in one lump sum per project on an invoice. At the time, sales tax was not required to be charged on labor, however, I had no way of checking to make sure the correct amount of tax was charged because materials and labor were not listed separately. I spent quite a bit of time going over the past projects with the owner of the landscape company. And he spent even more time going back in time to find out what materials had been used and purchased and how many man hours had been charged for each job.

One of the issues uncovered was that the mark-up on materials was not consistent. Mark-ups were anywhere between fifteen percent and twenty-five percent. I negotiated with the owner of the landscape company to only pay a ten percent markup. In my opinion, this was a fair deal; a win-win situation for both parties. A markup is fair because you don't have to spend your time looking for the best prices and buying the materials. If the contractor gets "contractor pricing" from his supplier, ask if he will pass that on to you—with the markup of course for his time.

Another issue corrected was the number of man-hours charged on the invoices. There was no reasonable explanation for the number of hours worked on a few of the invoices. For example, it doesn't usually take two persons five hours to repair a sprinkler head.

The owner made adjustments on the invoices that had already been paid, extended credits for those adjustments, and agreed to separate charges on all future invoices. The client was satisfied, the invoices were understandable, and the costs associated with landscape repairs were reduced. And the landscape company was still happy to have the account.

A manager's job is not to place a signature of approval on things he or she cannot justify. It is to provide justification for the approval and be sure that he is spending the client's money wisely. A detailed invoice provides that justification and, as shown here, provides information to confirm or question. Something as simple as having a contractor provide detailed invoices put more money in this client's pocket.

Make sure the invoices you approve have the following detail:

- A description of the work done.

- How many hours are included in labor—and make sure you agree with the number of people on the job and the hours it took to complete the job.

- A detailed list of materials used with charges broken out for each—don't accept "five sprinkler heads." Require the make, model, size, etc., so you know what was installed and have a record of it. This also permits you to check on the prices charged so you know if they are fair or not.

- The percentage of sales tax charged separated from all other charges. Should your sales and use tax ever be audited, the invoices will detail that you have paid the appropriate sales taxes. When sales tax is included in a lump sum for the job, it will not be apparent how much was charged or on what items it was charged.

For larger projects for which there is an approved bid specification document, the bid spec can be made a part of the invoice. The description of the work on the invoice could reference the bid spec. If an item on the bid spec was not completed, this can be detailed on the invoice as a credit. Likewise, if an item was added to the project, this can be detailed separately on the invoice with the accompanying charge.

As a side note: About a week after I told the client she could leave the research to me concerning the landscape invoices, she told me she knew when I got involved everything would be great again. I don't tell you this to pat myself on the back, but to make a point to you. Your client should be able to trust that you will serve them well. She should know that you care. If your client can't trust you to do the job and feels you don't care enough, they aren't going to keep you around very long. They certainly won't feel you are worth the fees you are charging them.

CHAPTER 7
IMAGE IS EVERYTHING

The first impression someone has of you or your business may be the lasting one. Only you can decide whether to make it a good one or not. Everything in your business presents an image; your confidence, the clothing you wear, your marketing materials, business documents and correspondence, your company website, and the people you hire.

Some of my perceptions:

- If you don't have confidence in your ability, no one else will think you are competent

- If you dress sloppily—people may think your work and business are sloppy

- If your lease is barely readable because it has been copied for the thousandth time—customers will think you don't care

- If your manager is surly and never smiles—they'll think you don't provide an enjoyable place to live or work

- If a staff member sends emails without punctuation or capital letters—it gives the impression that you don't train your people very well

WHO DO YOU WANT TO BE?

You should like yourself, feel good about what you do, and be proud to acknowledge the position you have. I don't meet many people who don't care about having at least some authority and recognition.

Years ago I took a required real estate continuing education class. The instructor was the best I ever had. Property management had been the topic most forgotten or brushed over in almost any continuing education class I ever attended. As in most cases, the property management portion of this class didn't take much time. In real estate, selling and investing are the most important. Property management is the two-page chapter at the end. But this time, the instructor said something so profound, I have never forgotten it.

As a property manager, you work with real estate and have a real estate license to do so. A property manager is part of the real estate industry, which requires you to know how to sell and how to manage. So why do you call yourself a property manager? Be proud of the industry you represent and be proud of yourself—you are a *Real Estate Manager*. You manage *Real Estate*!

When I started calling myself a real estate manager, I no longer was asked the question, "What is a property manager?" Now I heard, "Oh, you are in real estate!"

Think that would make you feel better about what you do? It made me feel really good. Real estate is a term almost everyone understands.

WHAT'S IN A TITLE?

First, a title is one of the first perceptions others have of you; residents, vendors, contractors, representatives of companies you do business with, attorneys, governing officials, etc. A supervisor or manager is automatically thought to have more authority than a technician or assistant. A director or vice president more than a supervisor or manager. And so on. Funny how things get done more quickly when people think they are doing business with someone with some authority.

Customers or clients will naturally feel more important and more in control of decisions made if they don't think they are speaking to the lowliest position on the organizational chart. It is all in the perception they acquire of the person they are speaking with.

Don't get me wrong here—every member of a staff is important. An organization cannot succeed without every position filled by someone who can do it well. This means that the perception of the person answering the phone is as important as the perception of the president the client is referred to.

We had a really wonderful woman sitting at the reception desk in our management office. She not only answered the phone and greeted customers and clients, she assisted in the administration department and basically managed the front office. In other words, we would not have been able to run our office without her.

I was walking through the front office one morning when she was on the phone. I heard her tell the caller she was *only* the receptionist and she couldn't help him. Thank goodness she also said she would find someone who could help him. I told her she should never tell anyone she was only the receptionist. She was so much more! Her response was that she thought of herself as the Director of First Impressions. In my opinion, she could be whatever she wanted to be—just not "only a receptionist."

It doesn't matter your position; don't degrade it. It is up to you to believe you are the best. If you don't, no one else will. I was told very early in my career that you have to create your own authority.

I learned a lesson here. Some staff members take their titles literally and may be unable to elevate themselves past the title or feel they don't have the right to do so. Thus, this person's title was changed to Office Manager. Please note, you don't want to use a title earned by executives of the company unless it has been granted to you.

Secondly, a title can create more confidence in the person who holds the title. When a person is thought of more highly by others, he naturally thinks more highly of himself.

A community of apartments and executive suites had a fairly lean staff. There was a manager who lived on site, an office assistant, housekeeping staff, and one maintenance tech. The manager supervised all positions. One day, the manager called me very upset. The maintenance tech wanted to be called—heaven forbid!—the Maintenance Supervisor and he didn't even supervise anyone. My response was, "So, let him be the Maintenance Supervisor." He handled every maintenance issue there was, he was on call twenty-four hours a day, he responded quickly, and the facilities were maintained immaculately.

If giving him a new title was all it took to make him feel good about his position, strengthen his loyalty, and ensure his continued employment, what was the difference? He didn't ask to work less hours, he didn't ask for more money, and he didn't complain. Letting him have the title he wanted changed nothing except how he felt about himself. We now had a team member who was proud of who he was and what he did. Despite the manager's fears, it didn't change her position or how her authority was perceived at all.

You choose who you want to be. I am betting you choose someone from Column B.

Column A	Column B
Maintenance Person	Maintenance Manager
Receptionist	Office Manager
On-Site Manager	Community or Resort Manager

Maintenance Manager	Facilities Manager
Property Manager	Real Estate Manager
Regional Manager	Regional Director
Owner	President, CEO, Chairman

If you work for a company that will not or cannot permit you to have some authority or represent yourself in an authoritative role, however minor it may be, then you may not be able to help choose your title. You can accept that and do the best you can or look for another company where you will be more comfortable. If you own a business and stifle your staff, then rethink how you manage them. How someone represents your company may depend on how they feel about themselves. The wording of a non-corporate title is important to morale; it doesn't change the organization or your company.

RESPECT YOURSELF!

You must respect yourself and believe you are worthy of respect before you can earn the respect of others. You know what the strengths are in your experience, abilities, and skills. You should never make jokes or negative statements that could reduce the value of your strengths. And never make jokes or negative statements about others. You will earn respect by respecting yourself and others.

In a 2007 episode of *The Apprentice*, Donald Trump "fired" one of the contestants for unprofessional behavior because he jokingly referred to himself as white trash. Trump expressed his displeasure over this "stinking," disrespectful statement, saying he'd never want anyone who willingly called himself white trash to work for him.

Outside of sporting events, I don't watch much television. This was the only episode of *The Apprentice* I have ever watched. I didn't think I would ever learn anything from a reality show, but this was a lesson for me.

How can a guy earn respect from others when he doesn't respect himself? If this guy makes negative remarks about himself, is he going to make equally or more offensive remarks about others? What others perceive you to be will ultimately come from you.

DRESS TO IMPRESS

I believe an essential part of your success is that your appearance is neat, clean, and presentable. Some companies have dress codes, some don't. This section is primarily for those who work with those that do not have any type of dress code. It is up to you to set your parameters and have pride in how you look and in what you do.

Picture this scenario and I kid you not, this happened: There are two multi-family communities each trying to attract the same target market and each has a female on-site manager. Both communities have approximately the same number of homes, similar amenities, comparable rents and the same number of staff. One manager dresses in old blue jeans, an oversized long-tailed shirt (never tucked in) and tennis shoes. The other manager dresses in dress slacks, silk blouse, a blazer, and dress shoes. Can you choose where you would live based on the manager's dress? Or if it is maybe a little too premature to make that decision, allow me to continue.

I visited both communities. When I drove through the community with the manager in blue jeans, I saw weeds growing around every structure and trash on some of the lawns. The clubhouse was unkempt and the restrooms were so dirty I elected to wait to get back to my office rather than use one. The person working in the office barely spoke to me but did get up to announce my presence to the manager sitting in her office. When visiting with this manager, I perceived a lackadaisical attitude and I heard about the issues she faced with non-paying residents, numerous police calls, and the difficulty in attracting new residents.

When I drove through the community with the manager in dress slacks, it was practically spotless. I was greeted in a professional and friendly manner by the person at the front desk and shown around the clubhouse and recreational areas, which were clean and inviting. When the manager was free and I was ushered into her office, I was offered a piece of cake left by the resident who had just left the office. The conversation was upbeat and the market outlook positive.

If you had visited both communities, where would you choose to live? At the lackadaisical, blue jean manager community or at the upbeat, nicely dressed manager community?

Dress sloppy, the business is sloppy!

Our company had a management account for an apartment community. Initially, the community was not in the best condition and the residents were not particularly happy with the management or the upkeep. One of the first things we did was hire a new on-site manager. He insisted on coming to the office every day in a shirt and tie. It wasn't a requirement, but he felt the residents would more quickly believe he was there to clean up their community if he personally portrayed that image. It worked! And when this manager had to perform some of the maintenance work, he put on a polo shirt and khakis.

This manager's appearance (along with the fact that the building and grounds were clean and groomed) made the statement, "I am proud to be here and I want you to be proud of where you live. "

Dress proudly!

To me, it doesn't matter what your profession is, you should dress accordingly. I was at an elementary school one morning and saw one of the teachers walk into the building. He was dressed in faded blue jeans with huge, stringy holes in each knee. Don't children look up to their teachers anymore? Are teachers not role models for children? Perhaps this is the style and the teacher purchased his pants in this condition, but, in my opinion, there is a time and place for clothing of this sort. It isn't for a professional setting.

If you are getting the idea I don't think old, ratty blue jeans provide the right image for elite managers—you would be correct!

Our office decided to implement Casual Fridays so everyone could dress more comfortably. The front desk attendant came to work the first Friday in a gray sweatshirt and sweatpants that were a couple sizes too large for her. At no time had we scheduled a morning workout for the office. Not a good image to portray to a customer who walked into the office. The attendant was sent home to change clothes. Unfortunately, this was a humiliating experience for her, but she didn't wear sweats to work again on Fridays.

In a professional setting, casual dress means business casual—not lying around the house or working in your yard casual. Business casual is less formal, but still gives a businesslike and professional impression. If you aren't sure what casual means, ask someone.

There are many businesses where casual wear is typical. Your favorite restaurants may have servers in shorts or pants and nice polos. Your veterinary office and doctor's office may have assistants in "scrubs." Your landscape company has employees in shorts and a shirt with the company logo. The convenience store you frequent has employees in shirts with the company logo. Casual wear has its place, but it is attractive and neat and can make a good impression.

The reason for requiring uniforms is that everyone working at the business is dressed to promote the business's brand and to make them noticeable as a member of the business's team. If you wear a uniform in your position, wear it proudly.

THE APPEARANCE OF PROMOTIONAL MATERIALS COUNTS, TOO

You want the assets you manage to compete with the best in the market. The documents and marketing materials for the assets must also compete. These are visible accessories to the dressing of the property, thus, are a reflection of the business and the asset. High quality materials will aid in attracting high-quality residents and tenants.

When I was still in Colorado, the company purchased its first property in Florida. Florida law required a prospectus be given to all homeowners in the property. The prospectus is the document that describes the major features and services of the property to prospective owners and outlines the rights of the homeowners and property owner and how land lease rents are increased. We had designed the presentation of documents for other properties, but this prospectus was new to us.

When I received a sample from the attorney in Florida, it contained many pages of writing on regular white paper. I was told the document was to be printed, stapled, and handed to prospective owners. This was not exactly in keeping with the image we had worked so hard to portray in all other properties over the years.

Unfamiliar with how things worked in Florida, I asked the attorney if the prospectus could be bound into a booklet with a glossy front and back cover that depicted the company's logo and branding image. After a brief pause, the attorney told me, yes, the document could be bound in whatever cover we desired as long as the required content was included. He then asked me why I would go to such expense for this document. He informed me no one else in the state tried to make the document pretty. My response was that it is all about the image. If you are the best, why give a fifty-page white and black document to someone when they can be handed a glossy booklet that shouts, "We are the best! You want to live here!"

But that isn't the entire story. What I thought was a five-minute phone call turned out to be an impression that lasted many years.

I lost touch with this attorney after the property was sold. Several years later I had the chance to meet up with him again when I was working with a company that owned several of the same type of properties in Florida. I was excited to make my first phone call to him and reconnect. While we were talking, he told me what he remembered most was that I wanted a glossy cover for the prospectus. He said I was the only one who had ever designed the prospectus as an attractive booklet. I thought I was only designing something to impress prospective customers. I do believe the most impressed person was the attorney advising us and what he remembered about the class act of the company he represented.

If the attorney you hire believes you are one of the classiest properties they have represented, what do your customers think? They may never tell you, but the answer may be in the quality of customers you attract and how many of them you attract.

Your materials don't have to be glossy. I have used matte-finish covers. Sometimes it depends on the photos and illustrations used.

Decide whether cotton or linen paper makes the best impression for what you are representing. Copy and multipurpose paper is less expensive but won't always make the best impression. Decide whether a color other than white is best. Cream colored paper is more formal, pastel is more fun. What are you trying to convey to your customers? The key is to figure it out and do something different than everyone else.

My husband performs instructional orientations for customers who buy RVs. Those RVs come with an extraordinary number of manuals for all the equipment and components in an RV. He organizes the manuals, places them in plastic sleeves, and identifies each for the customers. He has been told by customers no one else has ever done this for them. He didn't have to decide between glossy or matte, but he did decide he would give his customers a presentation few others provide, if any.

It is all in the presentation. Do you hand a bunch of papers to your customers for them to organize, or do you provide the papers in an organized manner in a folder in which they are contained?

When I first began working with an outdoor hospitality property, I found customers were being given numerous pieces of paper with instructions and information. You know what I do when I have a bunch of paper that becomes a mess on my car seat? I throw it away. I decided all this paper needed to be placed in a pocket folder. But what type of folder? I like things simple and I wanted only the property's bright red and green logo on the folder. Again, I had to decide between glossy and matte. The colors looked much better on glossy, so a glossy white pocket folder was ordered. Every piece of paper was placed in this folder in a specific order. It was a much nicer presentation of the material and it was organized. We received positive feedback after implementing the use of this folder. This folder helped improve the image of the property.

I have become involved in properties that have leases and other documents that have been copied so many times the wording on the pages is not straight and so blurry it is barely readable. Forget glossy or matte; at least make a clean copy of whatever you are giving out. I know I am pickier about these types of things than others, but what I would think if something like this were given to me is, "If you don't care about giving out crap like this, are you going to give a crap about me?"

WHO DESIGNS THESE WEBSITES?

Have you ever entered a website for a service you wanted to check out and found a black background with almost invisible text on it? Have you found the navigational tools on the site to be near impossible to figure out? Have you been unable to find the information you wanted? Were you expecting to find photos of the business and there were none?

You have a website so people can find your business. At the very least, a website legitimizes your business. If people can't read what is there or can't find the information they want, it really isn't worth the effort and costs you have put into the website to have it.

A website is one of the most important marketing tools you have. It needs to convey professionalism and communicate what you have to offer to others. It should have the image of your business you want people to remember.

Make sure your logo and any other branding information is prevalent and shown on every page of the website. Answer every question you think someone will have about your property. I loathe those websites that say, "Call for Pricing." If I wanted to call you, I would have done it before I looked at your entire website. You want the people who call you to be actual customers, if possible, so give them the rental or lease rates upfront. Don't waste the time of your personnel or the customer by having them call and find out they are no longer interested in what you have to offer because of the price. If you are afraid of losing customers before you get them or afraid of giving too much information to your competitors, then you need to rethink how you are doing business. You want to be the best and you want to be able to charge more than your competitors, so don't be afraid to market your property that way.

You want a beautiful website that gives as much information to a prospect as possible, and makes them want to call you. But you need to have a website designed so it can be found in internet searches. If keywords, search engine optimization, links, blogs, email capture, demographics, and the like are not your forte, you may want to hire professional help to make sure your website is noticeable.

IT'S NOT THE RITZ—BUT IT CAN BE

The first impression a resident or tenant has of a property may be the image the property itself gives as they drive in and through it. You, of course, want that image to make a positive impression. You and your staff dress professionally and look neat and clean. You should dress the property to look the same way; neat, clean, tidy, and attractive.

The following are areas where close attention should be paid.

- Signage needs to be up to date and in good condition, easy to find and read, and kept clean at all times.

- Streets, particularly at the entrance, should be free of potholes and weeds and swept free of debris.

- Grass should be mowed and landscaping trimmed.

- Make the entrance and high traffic areas "pop" by planting flowers and other attractive plants.

- Beautify the property when possible: paint, flooring, furnishings, appliances, bath and kitchen fixtures, etc.

- If there are recreational areas such as a swimming pool or sports courts, make sure they are maintained and kept clean and inviting.

- The entire property should always be clean and tidy.

The staff should follow a list of things that need to be done first thing in the morning when they get to work. For instance, the entrance is to be cleaned, the staff should do a trash run through the property to pick up anything a resident or tenant has thrown on the ground, and the recreational and common areas are to be cleaned and checked and made ready for the day.

Each time I visited a certain hospitality property in my portfolio, I noticed these things were not being done. The property did not look crisp and clean. Time after time I tried to make the manager understand his first responsibility was to present an attractive property that was free of trash and debris. On one occasion he looked at me and said, "This isn't the Marriott." Well, I already knew that, but it could have been with a little more care. What I was trying to accomplish, though, was to make the property comparable to the Ritz. We were such a long way off. Managers who settle for what exists because they don't want to work a little harder anger me. The owner of this property spent hundreds upon hundreds of thousands of dollars to provide quality amenities, yet the manager didn't want to maintain the property to show off those amenities. It is a manager's job to meet the goals and objectives of the owner. If the owner wants to improve the property and doesn't want to stay with the status quo, then the manager better get on board as well. A quality property attracts quality residents, tenants, and guests. As a manager you should understand that quality enables an owner to charge higher rates and fees, which equals higher compensation for the manager.

A property may not be the Ritz when you get it, but it can be if you put your mind to it.

CHAPTER 8
RISKY BUSINESS

An investor takes a financial risk when investing in real estate. That investor also bears a property loss and liability risk, which, if not managed properly, can have a significant negative effect on the financial resources of the investor. All in all, investing in income property with renters and lessees is a risky business.

RISK MANAGEMENT AND INSURANCE COVERAGE

It is very important that a real estate manager understands Risk Management as it pertains to the real estate being managed. Risk management is understanding the risks to property and financial assets and reducing the liability risk to the owner of the real estate. One accident can financially ruin an owner, so managing risk and maintaining safe premises are imperative for a real estate investor. A property should be maintained so there is little to no deferred maintenance. Risks are plentiful on any property, and they are considerably greater on a deteriorating property.

It would take a large book to discuss the many issues in rental properties that have resulted in lawsuits. There will always be something that happens that no one even considered a problem. There are, therefore, areas in the day-to-day management of a property everyone should be watching for.

- Swimming pools and spas: If required, the people maintaining your pool should have proper certification. Make sure chemicals are balanced correctly and the logbook is up-to-date and thorough. Don't just write down the readings from the chemical tests, write down when chemicals are added, when the filter is backwashed, when the pool is shocked (adding a great amount of chlorine), etc. With the high temperature maintained in spas, this is especially critical. It is not unusual for someone to blame the pool owner for skin irritation, stinging eyes, or respiratory issues. Having a good record of readings and maintenance could go a long way toward showing that management was not negligent.

- Fences and gates should, at the least, be maintained to code. Even better would be to have controlled access to the pool. Imagine the grief of the parents whose two children found a way to open a gate even though it was installed to code. The most painful claim ever filed on a property I managed was by the family of a child who drowned in that swimming pool and another who was impaired for life. The property was found innocent of negligence, but this was a very hard lesson in the fact that you need to take a detailed look at everything around you to determine if there is something that could be potentially dangerous to another to mitigate injurious situations. Security gates were installed at this pool so something like this would, hopefully, never happen to another family.

- Slip and fall issues: Repair uneven sidewalks, pavers that have settled, and uneven terrain. Turf areas should be checked to make sure there are no depressions and that all irrigation system-related valves, shutoffs, and the like are covered. Damaged flooring should be repaired or replaced. Pooling water can cause accidents, so find a solution to this problem. Common areas should be well lit.

- Safety: Make sure all doors and windows and all locks on them are in working order and that all ingress and egress areas of a building are accessible and working so no one is at risk of being trapped inside in an emergency because they can't get out or responders can't get in to help. Glass panels on entry doors should be shatterproof. Exit signs must remain illuminated and be tested often to make sure the backup system allows the sign to stay lit for at least thirty seconds in an emergency. At least once a year, the sign should be tested to make sure it stays lit for one and one-half hours in case there is a long-term emergency.

- Damaged asphalt: Damaged asphalt poses trip and fall hazards as well as risk of vehicle damage. Make sure the asphalt on your property is well maintained.

- Playgrounds: Equipment should be well maintained. Anything that could cause injury such as raised screws, peeling paint, cracks in structures, or worn ropes or chains should be repaired or replaced. Playground surfaces should meet the code in your area and be of a type and depth that will reduce injuries to children.

- Handicap access: If your property is required to provide handicap accessibility, make sure it is to code and in working order.

- Screening residents and employees: Managing risk isn't all about the physical components of the property itself. A background check should be conducted for all residents and employees of your company. This will reduce the risk of the owner being held liable for the unlawful acts of others.

Having proper and sufficient insurance coverage in place for the properties and employees you manage is a major part of risk management. It really annoys me when I hear a manager say they will let the people in the insurance department take care of insurance. Someone else in your company may put all the coverages in place, but how will you manage them if you don't understand them?

Insurance covers most of the risks and, in most cases, defends against liability. In order to properly manage risk, the real estate manager should have an understanding of what coverage is in place, how values are determined, and what happens when someone gets hurt on a property. Understanding the coverage helps a manager be cognizant of the risks that can be present on a property.

When I started with the first real estate management company, where I would spend twenty-four years, I learned during the first week I was to be in charge of insurance. The meeting with the insurance agent was the next week! Insurance? I only knew how to call my personal agent and get car or home insurance. I had to ask what kind of insurance we would be discussing at the meeting. It was insurance for the properties, but I didn't even know what that meant.

I looked through the files and found the policies. It was all foreign to me. I took the policies home and started reading. If you have trouble going to sleep at night, read your property's insurance policy and you will no longer have a problem. I am not sure I have studied anything more boring. I read about building and liability coverage. I found exclusions like war and flood and found out an umbrella isn't only to keep the rain off of you.

I entered the meeting with the agent only a tiny bit smarter. At least I could follow the conversation. But I knew I still didn't understand much. I had numerous conversations with the agent, asking question after question. Then came workers' compensation insurance and group insurance and the questions started again. It took me over a year to fully understand insurance coverage. After that, I knew what to look for and questioned some of the coverages we had. I was able to arrange for additional coverages that were needed and have some coverage removed, as it was not. I even learned how to negotiate premiums.

Insurance is purchased to protect the property (and therefore the investors) and those working at the property in case someone is injured or dies. The insurance companies have processes in place to determine what coverage they will offer on specific types of properties. The premium charged by the insurance company is based on the amount of risk or exposure to the insurance company. You need to understand all that to effectively manage risk.

SURPRISE! HE'S YOUR STATUTORY EMPLOYEE.

Pay close attention. He may not be your employee, but then again he might be according to your worker's compensation insurance carrier.

I acquired the management of a condo conversion/apartment community several years ago. After a couple of weeks, I determined the manager living on site had to be removed from his position. Contrary to my recommendation to terminate him from his position immediately, the owner of the property wanted to give him notice and let him continue to work until he found another place to live because he had been the manager for so long.

I should preface the rest of this story with the statement that staff at properties managed by our management company were employees of the property's ownership entity, not of the management company. Each property had its own payroll and maintained its own insurance coverage, including worker's compensation insurance.

After Sean (not his real name) had been given notice of his termination, he did some odd things. Things so out of the ordinary that residents in the apartments would notify my office of them. The last was the most bizarre. I received a call one day that Sean had been taken to the hospital because he fell from a second-story balcony. After investigating, this is what I found out.

Sean was scaling the outside of the building. Hand over hand, foot by foot, he made his way up the brick façade of the building. When he made it to the second story, he lost his footing or handholds or whatever and fell to the ground. When he was asked what he was doing he said he locked his keys in his apartment and was climbing up to his balcony to get in. He lived on the fifth floor!

To me, this was a red flag waving frantically in the air.

Of course, he filed a worker's comp claim and the worker's comp carrier accepted and processed the claim. When the carrier learned Sean's employer did not have worker's comp coverage, they placed the claim on our management company's policy. Note: We had learned the property owner did not carry worker's comp coverage shortly after we acquired the account and arranged for this coverage—but not before Sean's fall.

I tried unsuccessfully to have the claim denied because Sean was not our employee. I was told that because the management company controlled the employee and the actual employer did not have coverage, Sean was covered under the management company's policy as a statutory employee. I was taught that a statutory employee was defined as an independent contractor who worked for one company and, for tax purposes, was considered an employee of that company. I guess it is different with worker's comp. Make sure your company has adequate worker's comp coverage, even if you don't employ the staff at properties you manage. You never know when you will be held liable.

This I will never, never forget. When I was arguing the management company's position with the carrier, I asked why we were on the hook for a claim when the injured was stupid to try to scale the outside of the building. Their response was, and I quote, "We pay for stupid."

Although the employer is required to pay for worker's compensation coverage, it is in place for the protection of the employee, not the employer. It pays for legitimate claims for injured employees and it pays for stupid acts by employees. I learned to manage this risk more effectively after this incident.

Employees are as large a risk factor in real estate management as the raised sidewalk or pothole in the parking lot. I began workplace safety training and performing safety inspections. Within a week of completing this training, I went into an apartment home in the process of "make ready" for move-in. The maintenance tech was standing on a five-gallon paint bucket working on a light fixture in the ceiling. I asked where his ladder was and he told me he didn't want to take the time to go to the shop to get it. Needless to say, I took the paint bucket and the tech went to the shop to get the ladder and resumed his job. A worker's comp claim can increase the premium paid by the employer. Do your job correctly and make sure everyone working for the employer does their job correctly, uses proper tools, and uses safety equipment to reduce the risk of injuries and higher premiums. It is your responsibility to do so.

WHAT WAS HE THINKING!

Student housing management is a subject that could fill a book all on its own. We aren't going to go there, however, because this subject is risk management.

You think you have everything under control. The rules are in place. Students have been checked in. Parents have signed that they will responsible for their children. You offer great accommodations and amenities and plan to make more money this year than ever. Business is looking good. Then within the first week after the students come back to town, someone tries to dive into the pool from their third-floor balcony. Yep. Alcohol was involved.

The guy stands up on the railing of the balcony and jumps to the pool. Only problem is he misses the pool and hits the deck. Ownership and management feel for the guy. But guess what. The owner and management company get sued because the railing was low enough for him to get up on and jump, which caused his injury.

How do you plan for this type of risk? I don't think you can. The railings were installed to code. Years later the code changed to make railings two inches higher, but generally, an owner isn't going to replace every railing in a large property and he isn't expected to. Does anyone really expect a student to jump from the third floor to the pool and would two inches really have made a difference?

The trial for the case began. The property was not at fault and we felt the evidence proved this. We were confident our side would win. During jury selection, the insurance company settled with the man who was injured. They said the cost of the trial and the possible verdict against the property could be more costly than the settlement. We didn't have a say in the decision because the insurance company makes the decision. Talk about frustrating.

Be as vigilant over a property as you can be and keep up to date on building codes. Your attention and knowledgeable recommendations will enable an owner to make informed decisions regarding the property. When a similar situation happens at a property you manage and there is a large claim you aren't able to fight and win, inferior management won't be the reason when you are attentive.

YOUR SOLUTION COULD BE A LAWSUIT IN WAITING

Several years ago, our company decided to use live traps to capture wild animals that were running freely through a property. We thought we had the perfect solution to reduce this problem that caused many resident complaints.

One morning management was notified by a resident that their two-year-old son had been bitten by a raccoon trapped in one of the traps and was in the emergency room with a negative reaction from the bite. A few weeks later, the property was served with a lawsuit. The raccoon was diseased and the child was seriously harmed by the bite.

The insurance company placed a $50,000 reserve on the suit, which was in place for quite a long time. This was a high reserve and indicated the severity of the lawsuit. It took a couple of years to settle the suit and the payout was more than the reserve.

No one thought about a two-year-old child walking around the common areas by himself and trying to play with a trapped raccoon. That is the problem. You don't always think about the things that can happen if they have never happened before.

The lesson of this story is that anything you do can get you in trouble, so think about it long and hard before putting an idea into motion. That idea may be a risk to the property, but even worse, it can also be a risk to life. It is worse yet when it is a young life.

FIND A VERY GOOD INSURANCE AGENT

What helped me when I first began my career as a real estate manager was that I was able to work with a very smart agent. He answered all my questions and took the time to teach me about insurance. Thank you, Brook, if you are reading this. Later on I met an agent who was also a real estate investor. He knew the coverages needed to protect his investments because he knew his investments. To me, the reverse would also hold true. A manager who knows the investment should be aware of the coverages needed to protect that investment.

Great agents are difficult to find. Interview them carefully before giving them your business. If you don't have an agent who educates you and helps you make decisions, then you can find a better one. You want an agent who tries to find the best deal out there for you, but doesn't always make recommendation on price alone. Your agent should make sure a property has the best coverage and explains what it is and why you need it. After all, the coverage is there to protect the assets, the employees, and the owner's financial investment.

My company recently acquired a new management account. I read through the policies to become familiar with them. From my initial research of the property, I found it was not in a flood zone and I could find no evidence of flood insurance coverage in the policies. I called the agent to confirm my findings.

When I told him I could find no flood coverage in the policies and I wanted to make sure it wasn't required, he told me he was sure there was flood coverage because every property in Florida needs it. I asked him to tell me where to find the coverage then. He called me back to let me know the property was not required to have flood coverage and there was no such coverage written for the property. Ask me if I felt real warm and fuzzy about this agent after this exchange!

I could have taken his word that there was flood coverage without reviewing the policies. We would have both been wrong, though. Hire an agent who cares enough to educate himself about specific properties and who will give you correct answers. Otherwise, you will be doing all the work—because someone has to do it to protect the asset.

CHAPTER 9
HOW DO YOU MEASURE UP?

You want to be a successful real estate manager and maximize your income potential. Real estate management is a sales business, so you want to be a great salesperson as well. You want to maintain property assets in excellent condition, increase profits, and provide customer service that exceeds expectations.

You can. But it all begins with *you*. Now it's time to find out just how good you are.

Score yourself on each of the following from one (really bad) to ten (excellent) to see how you measure up.

_____ **Your image.** Do you dress to impress and present a neat, clean, and put together look, or are you careless with your appearance and dress sloppily?

_____ **Your confidence.** Are you confident in your ability? Do you think highly of yourself? Do you know what you are talking about? If you aren't confident, no one else will think you are competent.

_____ **Your attitude.** Do you show respect and empathy? Are you responsive, positive and enthusiastic? Are you a Compassionate Cheerleader? Do you always smile!?

_____ **Your work ethic.** Do you do your best and take the time to do things right the first time? Or do you say "We can get by"?

_____ **Your sincerity.** Is your sincerity genuine or do you fake it?

_____ **Your knowledge.** Do you learn something new every day—to never stop learning and be resourceful in order to gain exceptional knowledge and skills? Do you know your job? Knowledge = $$$$$$.

_____ **Your compassion.** How kind, considerate, and generous are you? Do you truly want to help others? Remember, your customers can sense whether you want to help them or not.

_____ **Your respect for yourself.** Do you respect yourself and believe you are worthy of respect? Respect is earned, not given freely.

_____ **Your respect for others.** Do you respect and show consideration to your customers? Do you use a person's name, look them in the eye, and nod to show you understand what they are saying? Do you give your customers your undivided attention?

_____ **Your enthusiasm.** Are you positive? Do you have fun, and help others enjoy themselves? Do you instill enthusiasm and excitement in others? When you are positive, your customers will respond to you more positively.

_____ **Your service.** Do you provide exceptional service to your clients by maintaining high-quality assets and producing the highest possible return on their investment? Do you create customer loyalty? Do you treat clients and customers honestly and professionally?

_____ **Your communication.** Are you really listening? Do you listen to what someone is saying to you, or are you thinking of what you are going to say next? Are you able to convey your thoughts so they are understood? Do you ask for another's ideas or solutions?

_____ **Your ability to make decisions.** Can you make a decision without falling into the analysis paralysis trap? Do you make good, informed decisions? Do you own up to and learn from wrong decisions?

Add your scores together and see how you rate.

111 – 130 Outstanding! You will prosper in your career.

91 – 110 Very good. You will make it in no time.

71 – 90 You have potential but still have work to do. Take classes, learn from others, read books. In fact, read this one again. And you may want to work on your attitude and learn how to get along with other people.

0 – 70 You need to find another profession. You aren't cut out for this one.

Those who want to better themselves find a way. If you didn't want to work at being great, you wouldn't have read this book. If you have confidence in your greatness, you can be a remarkable real estate manager.

I wish you the best of luck in your career. I hope it is as enjoyable and educational as mine has been.

ABOUT THE AUTHOR

Marie Hamling has extensive experience and knowledge in real estate asset management, sales and marketing, the leisure and hospitality industry, mortgage origination and brokerage, finance and insurance, construction and design, acquisition due diligence, disposition of assets, financial budgeting, and reengineering. She is the Property Rescuer[SM]. Working smart and the willingness to learn and adapt are her keys to success.

Multistate clients have included banks; a national real estate firm owned by a Fortune 500 company; owners of small and large apartment communities, owners of commercial office space, executive hotel suites, retail businesses, self-storage units, manufactured home communities and RV resorts; and community and homeowners' associations.

Marie is certified by the Institute of Real Estate Management, holding the coveted Certified Property Manager (CPM®) designation. She is a licensed Florida Real Estate Broker and Community Association Manager and the Owner/President of Paradigm Real Estate Corp., a real estate management and consulting firm in Fort Myers. She is also a licensed Mortgage Broker and Loan Originator.

Marie cares about people, and she enjoys solving problems and helping fulfill the needs of clients. A quote from John Heywood

(d. 1580) became her lifetime motto: *"Nothing is impossible to a willing heart."*

Marie lives in the Fort Myers, FL, area with her husband Charlie. She loves to spend time with friends and family, golf, read most anything in print, and root for the Denver Broncos.

NOTE FROM THE AUTHOR

Thank you for taking your time to read this book. I hope you enjoyed it. If you did, I will appreciate it greatly if you would write a review of it for Amazon, so that others might decide to give it a read.

I would love to hear from you and hear your comments on this book. I would like to know the things you would like to see in my next book, and make improvements in this one where you think they are needed.

My contact information is:
Marie Hamling
marie@paradigmrec.com
www.paradigmrec.com

Feel free to get in touch with me so we can talk about what kept your interest—or didn't—and to see if I can answer any further questions you may have. Again, I appreciate the time you spent reading this book.

Now go learn something new today. You are never too smart and never too old.

Best regards,
Marie Hamling